Colorado's Hot Springs

Colorado's Hot Springs

Deborah Frazier George

PRUETT PUBLISHING COMPANY
BOULDER, COLORADO

First edition 1996. Second edition 2000
Printed in the United States
09 08 07 06 05 04 03 02 01   5 4 3 2

Library of Congress Cataloging-in-Publication Data

George, Deborah Frazier, 1948–
    Colorado's hot springs / Deborah Frazier George.—2nd ed.
      p. cm.
    Includes bibliographical references (p.) and index.
    ISBN 0-87108-908-4
    1. Hot springs—Colorado. I. Title.
GB1198.3.C6F73 2000
551.2'3'09788—dc20   00-036608

Cover design by Julie Noyes Long
Interior book design by Kathleen McAffrey, Starr Design
Maps by Janet Moore, Chamisa Mapping
Cover and interior photographs by Deborah Frazier George except
   where noted otherwise.

To those long gone who loved the hot springs.

To the Utes, who showed the weak and weary the healing waters—the Utes, the springs' first and best guardians.

To those who introduced me to Colorado, hot springs, and nature's wonders.

To those with whom I'm now sharing the marvels: Dave, Devin, and Derek George. And those children I want to teach to know such special places and protect them: Rachel and Ryan Frazier, Matt Riach, Leslie Lacy, Jaime and Reed Johnson, and children yet to be born.

To the wish that we will leave the hot springs as glories for generations to come.

Contents

Introduction

Hot springs are Colorado's ocean.

The bubbles whisper. The warm mist beckons. The humid heat embraces.

The state's infinite Rocky Mountain panoramas lack little—except a sea, an ocean, or some such grand expanse of water. Alpine lakes are spectacular and foot freezing cold. The hot springs enfold the visitor with balmy mist and soothing heat that dispel the frigid fingers of winter.

There's no disloyalty to Colorado's grandeurs in longing for the moody sea or the rhythmic sigh of waves on a shore. Perhaps it's a primal quest for the prebirth amniotic state or a cosmic yen to join the earth in balmy communion.

Within the hot springs' quiet and foggy corners is the ocean's gift: a muffling of noise and other sensory clatter. The mind wanders its own waterborne course of dreams, life puzzles, and fancies. The buoyancy takes over the burden of life's inevitable loads.

Neither as immense nor as threatening as an ocean, the springs are calm water enclaves, land-locked tidal pools, and sweet water cousins of the great salt seas.

Colorado's hot springs number in the hundreds, counting small seeps, tiny trickles, and "secret springs" with undisclosed locations. In Steamboat Springs and Glenwood Springs, the springs' count is more than 100, but most are to small to enjoy.

Colorado's large springs number ninety-three and are strewn like a pirate's treasure west of Interstate 25. The pages ahead chronicle the three dozen that welcomed guests in 1999.

The other sixty major springs are nearly all on private land and include those that feed small personal pools, boarded up

The Hot Springs of Colorado

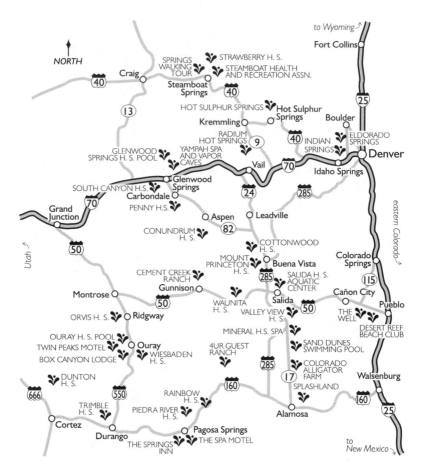

Legend

(25) Interstate highway	❧ Hot spring
(160) U.S. highway	○ City or town
(17) Colorado state highway	‿ Mountain pass
(134) County road	⛷ Ski area
FR 597 Forest Service road	▲ Campground
561 Trail	▲ Trailhead
Landmark peak	♫ Falls

commercial spas, or are plugged with cement to stop trespassing bathers.

The Colorado Geological Survey checks the springs every ten or so years and says there's been little change in temperature or minerals since they starting testing in the 1920s. The later surveys were done to assess geothermal energy potential in the state. Professional geologists share with simple soakers a curiosity about the springs.

Among the hot springs that are open to the public, there are six "people's" springs which are free—located on public land, undeveloped and primitive. Clothing is optional. There's Conundrum, Penny, Piedra, Radium, Rainbow, and South Canyon.

Of the commercially developed springs, only four charged more than $12 a visit in 1999. The hot springs are the last recreation bargain in a state of $55 ski lift tickets, $20 passes to amusement parks, and $10 parking tabs for professional sports.

Those uncounted springs beyond the official tally of ninety-three are the secret springs known only to locals and property owners and not listed in the geological surveys. They include the small pools alongside rivers, in cow pastures, and cause patches of blue ice on ski slopes. The location isn't disclosed to strangers. Fishermen sometimes stumble upon them as do rafters, hikers, and hunters. The pools often are on private land, so there's rarely a friendly welcome for trespassing bathers.

In 1999, at least five developed springs were closed and up for sale. The price for each, including buildings and surrounding acreage, ran about $1 million. The owners either have retired or don't have the financial resources to reopen.

For instance, Juniper Hot Springs, located west of Craig, has been closed since the 1980s when a proposed dam project threatened to flood the aging hotel, pools, and cafe. The dam idea was abandoned, but no one's bought the springs. A government engineer "located" Juniper Hot Springs in 1882—the year after the Utes were removed. An old photo from 1892 shows a small log structure surrounded by canvas tents.

During the late 1990s, at least one popular hot spring was bulldozed out of existence. In the past decade a half dozen or so hot springs on private land had met the same fate because owners wearied of lost cattle, trash, all night parties, and rude trespassers. And, the Iron Springs Spa in Glenwood was plowed out of existence along the Colorado River by its owner, a mining company. Iron Springs had opened in 1896 with the county sheriff as the owner. By 1939 there was a tourist shuttle to and from town. Bathing was twenty-five cents. In the 1940s, the *Saturday Evening Post* recommended the spa as one of the best places in Colorado. All gone.

On the other hand, two long-closed springs reopened for business since this book's first edition—the Sand Dunes Swimming Pool and Mineral Hot Springs. And Hot Sulphur Springs emerged from a major renovation as one of the nicest springs in the state. Three other hot springs have been sold and work started, but weren't ready to open.

There's a frontier independence to the springs and their guardians. There's no owners' association. The grapevine spreads word of sales, closures, and improvements, but visiting bathers tend to know more of the news than resident owners.

Each of the developed springs reflects the owners: the Glenwood Springs Hot Springs, Lodge, and Pool is owned by locals and run for the thousands who come each year—not sheer profit; the Desert Reef Beach Club near Cañon City melds the owners' environmental architecture with their humor; and Sand Dunes's owners near Hooper have children, so the pool is a kids' place.

Like the state's fifty-five peaks over 14,000 feet or the fourteen major rivers in Colorado, the hot springs are far flung. No two look the same or have identical minerals, but the water is always warm. And people have been soaking there for centuries.

History's Stage and Crystal Ball

Hot springs have been part of nearly every historical twist and turn in Colorado's past. Centuries before European explorers arrived on this continent, springs were used by Native Americans for rituals and ceremonies. Spirituality and steam were one. The waters were part of healing, strengthening, and affirming the life-giving connection with the earth. The Colorado Utes, and, later, Plains tribes shoved west by European settlers, cherished the waters as sacred. Each spring has Ute stories—given by elders to tribal members even today. The hot springs were among the last parcels of land the Utes surrendered.

Accounts written by nonhistorians in many hot springs towns describe the Colorado Utes "giving" the hot springs to settlers. Other stories refer to Native Americans leaving on an annual migration but mysteriously never returning. That's not what happened.

The Utes were removed, at gunpoint in some cases, by the U.S. Army in 1881. Homesteaders were right behind the cavalry, claiming farmsteads. Manifest Destiny, gold strikes, flight from the industrialized Northeast and the impoverished post–Civil War South, the railroads stretching west, and the tidal wave of immigration from Europe created pressures that broke treaty after treaty with the Utes. Both the territorial government and the U.S. Army ignored extensive squatting on Indian land long before 1881. "The Utes Must Go," echoed from Colorado's halls of government, church pulpits, and land speculation offices.

The Utes *did* go, in 1881, to two reservations in southwest Colorado and to one in Utah. The Utes didn't give the springs away or just leave. A powerful invader took the springs from them.

Native Americans still visit nearly every hot spring in the state, often in the off-season for privacy. The visits are often for spiritual, not recreational, purposes. Native Americans' connection to the hot springs and the spiritual realm they represent have endured despite years of exile and loss. Respect the first owners and their ceremonies as you would a Catholic, Jewish, Protestant, or Buddhist prayer service.

Those Who Came Later

Like the Utes before them, explorers, trappers, miners, and settlers sought solace in the soothing waters. The famed Frémont expedition, which mapped ore loads, drew in a few hot springs on the charts. Other explorers mapped Colorado's rivers and streams, the geology and the vegetation. The trappers used the information to find beaver, otter, and fox. The miners came in droves, answering the call of gold and silver. Part of the legacy each group left were the locations of hot springs.

All of the springs are in western Colorado and many are close to the mightiest gold finds, flowing fringe benefits for miners whose lives were spent beneath the ground in cold and wet. Glenwood Springs was founded by a Leadville miner, Isaac Cooper, who couldn't bear another year of the miserable dirty work. He proclaimed the hot springs a cure for all aches, pains, and respiratory problems brought on by mining and founded the town.

The early miners were among the first squatters around springs, pitching tents between cabin and spring for easy access. A few enterprising souls left mining to operate bathhouses and therapeutic pools. And there were settlers like James Crawford in Steamboat Springs, who opted for a homestead with a hot springs in the 1870s and profited by building a public bathhouse. By the early 1900s, Steamboat, Glenwood, Ouray, Pagosa, and other Colorado hot springs towns were part of the international spa circuit.

Soaks and Spas, Resorts and Radium

Pilgrims to Colorado hot springs in the 1900s drew on hundreds of years of tradition in Europe. The baths of England, the spas of Austria, and geothermals of Scandinavia were national treasures. Colorado hot springs were outposts on a worldwide tour. At Colorado's foremost hot springs spas—Waunita, Wagon Wheel Gap, Eldorado Springs, Glenwood Springs, and Pagosa Springs—there were lectures on literature and politics, music and dancing, and sometimes large doses of religion. Enlightenment was part of the spa experience.

As the United States sallied forth into the industrial age, the successful and the socially prominent modeled their lives on European culture. Spas with mineral hot springs and erudite activities were part of that sophistication. The pollution and disease that flourished in New York, Boston, Chicago, Baltimore, and other industrial cities made popular the venerable European prescription

Glenwood Springs in its early days. (Photograph courtesy Colorado Historical Society)

for "cleansing the body of impurities." In those last decades before antibiotics, influenza and pneumonia epidemics killed thousands in urban centers, with their open sewers and untreated water. A few weeks spent in the rarefied Colorado air, dosing oneself with pure mineral water, was a romantic tonic.

Even before the spa movement and the turn of the century, soaking in Colorado's hot springs was credited with curing cancer, baldness, arthritis, kidney disease, glaucoma, sterility, gout, mental illness, and asthma. Such powers sound far-fetched today, although there are lots of glowing testimonials from people claiming to be cured of their illnesses.

Besides bathing, doctors ordered springs-water injections, enemas, and poultices. Some regimes included drinking springs water by the gallon. There's no record that this hurt or killed anyone.

The spa movement didn't survive the Great Depression, although individual resorts such as Glenwood Springs and Eldorado Springs did. In the decades that followed, the hot springs resorts languished as American families took to the highways on vacation. A few resorts closed as vacation success came to be measured in miles traveled and states seen from the highway. Some, like the Box Canyon and the Twin Peaks in Ouray, and The Spa Motel in Pagosa Springs, adapted by adding motels.

Some say the hippies of the 1960s and 1970s saved many of the springs by enjoying them when it wasn't fashionable. The baby-boomer generation is taking over now, bringing their children and the early aches of arthritic joints.

The Geology of Hot Water

Hot springs are the earth's sweat. From fractures in the planet's rocky skin, steam and hot water billow. The Old Faithful geyser in Yellowstone National Park spews hot water skyward while hundreds of other hot springs in the Yellowstone Basin seep, sputter, and spout.

Japan has the highest number of hot springs, but Europe, Russia, China, Canada, Scandinavia, New Zealand, and the United States are well blessed. To qualify as a hot spring, water temperature must be at least 90 degrees Fahrenheit. Colorado's hottest is Mount Princeton, at 182 degrees.

The hot springs water comes from rain and snow that trickle down far beneath the earth's surface. There, the runoff fills deep cavern reservoirs. Deeper still a molten core burns—the volcanic magma that formed the planet billions of years ago. That enduring molten core heats the runoff in the underground chambers. The water boils, swells in volume, and sends off steam. And the hot water shoots to the earth's surface through faults, breaks, and fractures in the layers of rock. To complete the cycle, the spent water meanders back down again below the surface.

When the geologic plumbing is right and tight, there's a geyser spouting water skyward. Colorado has no Old Faithful, although there once was a small geyser that puffed rhythmically and gave Steamboat Springs its name. Regrettably, blasting for the railroad in the early 1900s sank the Steamboat geothermal and its throaty chugging sound. Hot springs, on the other hand, have a steady flow, are less spectacular, and not quite as hot—the water doesn't stay close to the magma long enough for superheating or else cools on the upward journey.

As the steaming water speeds upward through the underground corridor of faults, the flow picks up minerals from the rock layers it passes through: carbonates, chlorides, sulfates, and the like. Once the water erupts on the surface and cools, the minerals often drop out to form agate-colored basins and terraces around the springs. Mammoth Hot Springs in Yellowstone, with its terraces upon terraces upon terraces, is an example of note. Owners of commercial hot springs rue high mineral concentrations, which clog pipes and slowly coat pools. Pagosa Springs, the caves at the Indian Springs in Idaho Springs, and the subterranean chambers at the Yampah Spa and Vapor Caves in Glenwood Springs all show heavy mineralization.

The menu of minerals found at various Colorado hot springs is varied: sodium, potassium, iron, boron, magnesium, silica, zinc, selenium, phosphorous, and fluoride. The Colorado Geological Survey examines the minerals every ten years or so. Salt tops the list in terms of sheer volume—440,000 tons of salt a year at Glenwood Springs alone. A few springs have a little arsenic, but not enough to matter. Others have a touch of lithium—used to make the well-known antidepressant—but not enough to change your mood.

The springs in the wild and in places such as Yellowstone have created unique temperature-controlled ecosystems. At each, the water's temperature determines what will grow in it. In Yellowstone and on the Springs' Walk in Steamboat Springs, each spring's temperature and mineral combination support algae endemic to that geosystem.

There are hot springs in many states, although the West and Arkansas are especially well sprung. The flatlands of Texas, the high deserts of New Mexico and Arizona, and the Pacific Northwest boast lovely springs. The Rocky Mountains are ideal hot springs territory. The jamming and ramming of ancient mud, ash, clay, gravel, and sand layers eons ago bent, buckled, and ripped the mountain surfaces. There are fractures galore for funneling water down to the volcanic core and, once it is heated, back to the surface.

Although made of stone, hot springs are fragile and their plumbing is finicky. Highway construction has snuffed springs in

Steamboat and Glenwood. Experiments with geothermal heating rattled the springs in Ouray. However, Ouray, Pagosa Springs, and some other hot springs towns have successfully tapped the heat energy of their springs without damaging the geothermal system. Elsewhere in Colorado and the world, hot springs have been harnessed to grow flowers and fish, heat homes, and generate electricity.

Springs worldwide have died after being stuffed with trash. From Yellowstone's spectacular geothermal features rangers have extracted furniture, petticoats, toilet paper, coins, and other tokens of appreciation. The flows always improve after the cleanings. Although workers pull false teeth, jewelry, and a bounty of hair clips from the filters at Colorado's developed springs, the mother spouts are usually fenced and protected.

There's no such security for the primitive, undeveloped places. Only the kindness of strangers and backcountry etiquette guard their founts. And as Colorado's wilderness springs draw more people to their pools, the visitors' manners will determine the future of the springs. The Golden Rule is a good place to start.

Health and Hot Water

The Greeks and Romans swore by the invigorating power of hot mineral water, building stone baths in their empires' remote reaches. Cleopatra wallowed in the warm water, convinced that she emerged from it younger. The Japanese, endowed with more hot springs than any other nation, worked steam baths into social and religious rituals. The Scandinavians, Native Americans, Europeans, and British were blessed with geothermal outpourings and learned early that a good soak cleared the mind, cleansed the body, and recharged the spirit. The early Christians preferred warm springs for baptisms. And Ponce de Leon searched in vain for the spring of eternal youth.

For 150 years Colorado's hot springs have been touted as curing sicknesses of the body and mind. For early settlers, a hot bath at least improved on personal hygiene. A few hours in a piping hot pool eased aches and injuries sustained in the Civil War, hardrock mining, railroad building, and homesteading. Soaking *does* make people feel better. But as a cure for cancer, rheumatism, infertility, sterility, emphysema, epilepsy, and dozens of other diseases the springs were said to vanquish: no. Many claims were publicized by some of the springs' developers, who were bent on more business, not accuracy in advertising.

The worst—and the most erroneous—claim made about Colorado's hot springs involved radium. In the early 1900s, physicists Marie and Pierre Curie discovered the extraordinary properties of radium, including the ability to make X-ray photographs.

The same people who swore by snake oil and saw "leeching"—letting large sluglike creatures suck large quantities of blood from the sick—as a cure-all fell in love with radioactivity. Radium-coated drinking glasses were a health hit. Watches with the numbers painted in radium were said to prolong life. And so several Colorado hot springs added "radium" as a proud surname until the era ended abruptly in the 1920s, when radium's lethal side effect surfaced—cancer.

The "radium" springs took the signs down. There'd been no radium in the water anyway.

Today, claims of miracle cures from iron or sulfur or phosphorus are out. Hygiene is in. County health departments inspect public hot springs at least once a year. When there are complaints, an inspector usually makes a special trip. The state health department keeps an eye on the inspections, the complaints, and the springs.

All big public pools use chlorine or bromide or ozone filters to keep the water clean. Most springs have a good water flow that refills pools every twelve hours or so. Pool managers maintain regular routines of scouring, disinfecting, and steam cleaning. Which isn't to say every pool, steam room, or vapor cave is germ-free every minute of every day. After swimming or lolling, a shower with a good soap-scrubbing is a wise idea, if only to remove minerals.

So look around. Chances are, you'll find everything is clean. If not, think twice about taking a dip. "If you see green growths, it's not a good sign," says Glenn Bodnar, who supervises hot springs for the Colorado Health Department. "They're wonderful places when they're clean."

Here's one warning: Don't drink the pool water. Especially not in the primitive springs. YOU know why. *Giardia*, for instance. This waterborne bacteria causes what is known as "backpackers' disease." Hours of severe cramps, nausea, vomiting, and diarrhea. The coliform bacteria from human waste can be worse. Get the picture?

However, some springs provide mineral water at special faucets. This water is safe to drink.

A few other presoak warnings: People with high blood pressure and heart problems should check with a doctor before soaking in a hot spring. Children in hot pools should be monitored carefully for signs of too much exposure to heat. And at Colorado's high elevations, the sun gains in intensity. A goodly dab of sunscreen on your face won't sully the water, but it will help prevent serious sunburn.

There are rules against hot springs' owners making claims about the water's medicinal effects, but holistic healers and alternative medicine missionaries attribute improved circulation to iron, lessened joint pain to sulfur, and credit calcium with calming nerves and soothing muscle aches. These are intriguing claims, but the fact is that human skin does not absorb minerals in any significant volume. The warmth and relaxation gained from soaking are worthy therapies, however.

It's More than Hot Water

Sojourners of Colorado's hot springs have sought warmth and comfort. Some credited the water with power over disease and even death. It is certainly true that no one is hurt by a day of repose in a hot spring, with mountains, forests, and rivers as backdrop.

The habitués of hot springs are, by nature, seekers. Whether seeking refuge from cold or pain or stress, bathers seem to crave more than hot water. Conversations at hot springs are rarely about sex or sore muscles. The talk is about faith—a belief in something greater than individual intelligence: crystals, herbs, Buddhism, basic Christian fundamentalism, rigorous Orthodox Judaism, massage to release the spirit, all flavors of psychotherapy, and on and on.

Maybe the talk is part of the walk into the water—the relaxed mind seeking a higher plane. Bathers prone to taking the cerebral approach to any and all pleasure point out that solitary immersion in hot springs pools recreates the prebirth state: warm, safe, and enveloped by the bliss of the unknowing. Perhaps. But those who have partaken of the springs' warmth know that the surest tonic has always been the water's ability to soothe away the pain Shakespeare's Hamlet described as "The slings and arrows of outrageous fortune . . . That flesh is heir to."

Which brings us to hot springs' ethics.

As more people visit springs, in part because of books such as this one, the springs—both the wild and the developed—are at the mercy of the bathers. Care for them well and mentor others on leaving the trees, rocks, flowers, and grasses untrampled.

At stake is the scene at the springs that took your breath away when you first gazed at the water and the sky. The springs are yours to care for too.

Strawberry Hot Springs

44200 County Road 36
P.O. Box 773332
Steamboat Springs 80477
(970) 879-0342
Open to the public; no credit cards; limited camping and cabins; semiprimitive
Where: From U.S. 40 (Lincoln Avenue) through Steamboat Springs, turn northeast on 7th Street. Meander through a residential area to Park Road. Turn north (left) and continue north on the winding, rolling dirt road for about 8 miles. Four-wheel-drive vehicles are required in winter. Shuttles, available in town in the winter, are recommended.

A warm inland tidal pool in an idyllic mountain valley. The necklace of pools breathes steam in the early morning as if answering the rising sun and the perfect day ahead. Small water falls and rock walls separate the ponds of varying temperatures. The sandy pool bottoms comfort sore feet.

Set on a parcel of private land that's at 7,500 feet above sea level within the Routt National Forest, Strawberry is located in an aspen-studded valley. Deer, fox, dozens of bird species, and a host of creatures also inhabit the valley and leave hoof and paw prints in the sand around the pools.

Steamboat Springs Area

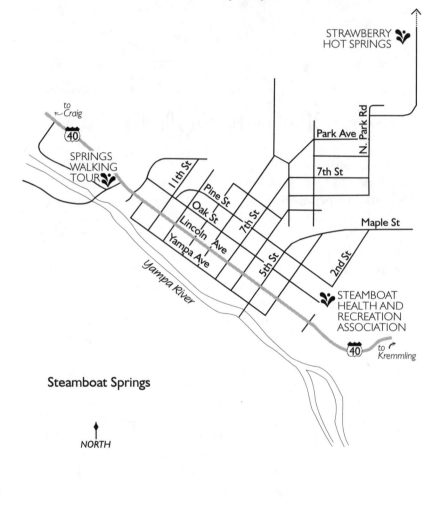

Small waterfalls abound at Strawberry Hot Springs.

The springs sputter to the surface at up to 147 degrees, perfect for making soft-boiled eggs. The current owner prohibits cooking in the springs, but early photographs of the place show visitors cooking fish, beef, eggs, tea, and vegetables.

The spring water has far higher uses that cooking.

The alpine refuge attracts seasonal tides of skiers, hunters, young families, overexercised summer visitors, and New Age believers in search of the universe's center. There are five small cabins and six tent sites, which share a small common bathroom and shower for the lucky few who call ahead for overnight reservations.

When the sun tops the mountain ridge, the morning light turns the billowing vapor incandescent. The steamy flow pours, glittering over the pools. The waterfall of mists moves in slow motion in the absolute quiet of morning and vanishes when the sun warms the earth to match the steam's hot whispers. It's a show worth rising early to catch.

Local lore claims the Ute Indians used the hot springs after battles with other tribes to heal body and soul. The Utes believe now, as they did hundreds of years ago, that the vapors contained their creator's essence and soaking in the pools rejuvenated the soul.

Starting in the the 1870s, settlers and miners claimed the land and ousted the Utes. And each owner, except the current one, lost the fight to protect the springs from boisterous and destructive marauders. The Utes were disgusted with the whites' trash and inattention to sanitation. From the first white owner until the current one, the keeper of the springs' fought trespassers and wild parties.

The original homestead family survived $24 per head cattle prices, foul winters, and desperate economic times, but years of ousting uninvited guests made them delighted to sell the springs to the Steamboat Springs Health and Recreation Association for $1 in 1936.

The alpine bacchannalia continued throughout the 1970s because there was no regular supervision. The county sheriff had the unwelcome task of breaking up fights, shutting down drunken parties, and answering neighbors complaints every weekend until 1982 when the current owner, Don Johnson, bought the property.

Don's offer to the recreation association came amid public discussion of bulldozing the springs or selling the land to a national hotel chair that wanted to build a resort. Instead, volunteers built the pools, Don hauled off trash by the truckload and chased off biker gangs, transients, and insistent party seekers.

The rest is magic.

Don has sculpted pools, built cabins (including one for the resident masseuse and one for the caretaker), landscaped the hillside to look natural, and started work on a sauna. Don is a former Chicago entrepreneur.

"A lot of people worship this place, and it's an important place for them," said manager Sunshine Davis.

In the last few years, Strawberry has added a full bathhouse with massage therapy. There's a changing tepee, which adds a Native American touch to the springs and a dirt path that goes halfway around the rock-rimmed pools. The upper pool, which measures about 30 feet by 100 feet, is usually 104 degrees, and the lower pool, 15 feet by 20 feet, is about 102 degrees. There are hot

Winter at Strawberry Hot Springs.

pockets where other springs flow into the pool. And for refreshment, steps take the bather down to a pool where an icy mountain stream is only slightly warmed by a spring.

Strawberry is a primitive hot spring in that there's no electricity. Don reluctantly added a telephone a few years ago only because his neighbors complained about stranded motorists—all without four-wheel drive or chains—pestering them during the winter. There's a section of the road that's called the Luge Run, full of twists, turns, and plunges. And the neighbors tired of digging people out, so now the county has a $500 fine for any inexperienced winter driver who gets a vehicle stuck on the road—even a SUV with studded tires.

For those without trucks and chains, there are shuttle services to Strawberry that run from Steamboat. In 1999, there was the Strawberrie Park Hot Springs Tour, (970) 879-1873 or 879-8065 or www.windwalkertours.com; Sweet Peas Tours at (970) 879-5820; or for a higher price, Alpine taxi at (970) 879-TAXI.

Like other springs with minimum development, Strawberry doesn't advertise. Friends tell friends. Folks come back every few years. And there's the feel of a private club bound by love of a special and largely undiscovered natural treasure. But not everyone "gets it."

"We're cracking down on obnoxious behavior, which is worse on busy weekends," said Sunshine. "We want a natural eden with relaxation and calm. Every year, we get a little more quiet. The rowdies are more of an occasional nuisance that a general problem."

As a result Strawberry may go to a no-alcohol policy. "Drunks are already banned," she said. And any guest who reports another bather using a glass container receives a free pass for another day.

The five cabins are rustic—a carpeted floor and a raised, wooden platform, which is also carpeted. There's a propane heater and a lamp. On each porch is a small cooking grill and two plastic lawn chairs. The cabins and most of the six tent spaces are set back in the woods, hidden from the pools. There are two deluxe cabins that have gas fireplaces, a kitchenette, and a bath. The two gypsy wagons feature only a light and a double mattress. The roof is canvas, and it's bring your own sheets and towels.

On a summer afternoon—or a winter day before the crowd arrives—Strawberry Hot Springs has the look of a trout habitat for humans. The water is dark and smooth. Sunlight wafts through the trees. People float nearly submerged in the water, and soft conversation is the only sound. Because of the high temperatures, youngsters usually prefer the Steamboat Springs Health and Recreation Association's swimming pool in town which has a water slide.

After dark, when the day trippers have left, the clothing optional rule goes into effect. Couples stay close and, perhaps, discuss spawning.

The setting eventually quiets the inevitable boisterous group. A zillion stars flicker above. The tendrils of mist shroud the couples embracing in the pools' far corners. The water is obsidian black on the surface, but clear to the sandy bottom if you look down.

Imagine floating in warm silk.

Steamboat Springs Health and Recreation Association

136 Lincoln Avenue
P.O. Box 1211
Steamboat Springs 80477
(970) 879-1828
Open to the public; credit cards accepted
Where: In Steamboat Springs, U.S. 40 becomes Lincoln Avenue. The Steamboat Springs Health and Recreation Association's facilities are located on the southeast side of town—toward the ski resort—on Lincoln Avenue/U.S. 40. The complex is on the north side of the road. See map, page 2.

There was a bathhouse for these springs before there was a town. Today, the Steamboat Springs Health and Recreation Association runs a warm water complex consisting of one large swimming pool with a large shallow end for children, a winding loopy water slide, three hot soaking pools, tennis courts, a fitness club, gardens, and picnic areas on the grounds of the original bathhouse. The pools are all outdoors. There's something for everyone with enough room in between, and there's no crowding.

Long before the high-speed chairlifts, gondolas, and skiing, the ranching community of Steamboat Springs grew up around the 150 hot springs in the broad Yampa River Valley in northwestern Colorado. Today the swimming and soaking pools in the Health and Recreation Association's complex are as much a part of the town's social life as were the series of bathhouses that anchored the early community.

In the summer there's a rodeo every week, hot-air balloon rides most mornings, trail rides, hiking, biking, fishing, golf, gondola

The pools at Steamboat Springs Health and Recreation Association are tailor-made for family fun.

rides to the top of the ski area, rafting, boating, concerts, theater, and dozens of other activities. Downhill skiing is the most popular winter sport, but the area has excellent cross-country skiing, sleigh rides, elk feeding, snowmobiling, and other cold-weather activities.

It all started at the hot spring.

In bygone times, the Yampatika Utes camped at the same spring, located on a small mesa about 100 feet above the Yampa River. Contrary to contemporary translations, *Yampa* doesn't mean "healing waters." Instead, it means carrotlike vegetable. Not very romantic, but the wild vegetable *was* a diet mainstay for the Utes throughout Colorado and Utah.

Before the U.S. broke the treaty that deeded northwest Colorado to the Utes, the first settler in the area, James Crawford, built a bathhouse in 1875 at the Steamboat Springs Health and Recreation Association's current site. The previous year he had found the spring, later named Heart Spring, while hunting, and he sped back to the family homestead a half-mile away. Crawford loaded his wife, three children, and his parents in a wagon, drove back to the spring, where he'd dug a hole that filled with hot water from the geothermal spout, and the family enjoyed a rare warm bath.

Crawford told later settlers that a Yampatika Ute leader known as Yarmony or Yahmonite recounted a battle he'd witnessed between the Utes and the Arapahoes when he was a child. The Utes were camped below the spring on an island in the river. One night a band of Arapahoes crept up behind a hill overlooking the island and surprised the Utes with their attack. Yarmony told Crawford he had seen his own father killed in the fight over control of the area's springs. Long before the Europeans, other Indian bands sought sovereignty at the springs. In Yarmony's time, about 1850, the Utes and the Arapahoes weren't allies.

H. W. Gossard, who owned the property between 1931 and 1935, named the spring Heart Spring, for its shape. Gossard added a second story to the bathhouse and introduced the winter carnival, a tradition that continues today, and it featured a local man diving into the pool from atop a 100-foot ladder. Successive owners built successively larger bathhouses from logs and native stone.

In 1935, Gossard's Steamboat Springs Co. sold the springs to the Health and Recreation Association for ten dollars. The association opened the pools to the public.

Old pictures feature flappers from the 1920s in swimming outfits so modest that they included bathing socks. A photo from 1913 shows an elk swimming across the pool, and a 1947 picture of a spring festival captures a skier flying into the pool.

A flagstone-and-river-rock basin catches Heart Spring's flows today. That pool, of course, is heart-shaped. The crystalline water in the pool is about 102 degrees, the same temperature as the hot spring itself. The spring fills the main swimming pool, the spa pool, and another hot soaking pool.

Steamboat is still a town where a trip to the grocery store can take more than an hour because one is constantly running into friends. Going to the swimming and soaking pools means talking to friends. Unlike some other fast-growing Colorado resorts, Steamboat Springs remains a place where locals outnumber newcomers and still welcome new people into the community.

Occasionally, one of the hot soaking pools will fill with people. Not because the other pools are full, but because the soakers all know one another and want to talk. The pool takes on the atmosphere of an intimate cocktail party where everyone is laughing, chattering, and having a good time.

In the spirit of community, locals can work off the cost of a yearly membership pass. Volunteers help run the day-care center, maintain the extensive landscaping, and keep up with repairs.

"My favorite scene is people arriving. They're tired, their children are whining," says association director Pat Carney. "They soak and sit and sun and they leave and they're happy. You can watch the transformation. It's so nice to be doing something where what you do makes people feel good."

A Walking Tour
of the Springs of Steamboat

Seven springs: 2 miles, 2 hours
No charge; no bathing; don't drink the water
Where: In Steamboat Springs, U.S 40 becomes Lincoln Avenue. The Springs Walk starts at the northwest side of town at 13th Street and Lincoln. There are parking lots on 13th Street, on both sides of Lincoln Avenue. Start anywhere—the trail is a loop. Maps are available at the chamber of commerce booth at 1255 North Lincoln Avenue, one block from the Springs' Walk parking lots. See map, page 2.

There's lots of talk about hot springs, but only Steamboat Springs has a self-guided hot springs walking tour.

A 2-mile trail meanders from Heart Spring at the Steamboat Springs Health and Recreation Association complex on the east side of town to six springs at the west end of town. A brochure is available, with a map, at the Steamboat Springs Chamber of Commerce building near the walking tour's parking lot or at the other end of town, at the Steamboat Springs Health and Recreation Association's pool complex.

The route winds along the river and through town parks, all perfect for picnics. The Howelson Hill ski jump towers above the trail, and winter practice jumps send skiers high into the air. It's a show worth stopping to see.

More than 150 hot springs percolate to the earth's surface near Steamboat. Some are on private land and closed to the public. A few are well-kept secrets. Some are tiny seeps in hay fields.

The seven along the walk offer a unique glimpse of geology and thermal energy—it's like a stroll through a geomorphic flower garden. And it's open every day, all year, for free.

Unfortunately, you won't need a lemon anymore.

Earlier in this century, before soda pop was invented, locals sliced up lemons on hot summer days and made lemonade at Soda Spring. The water was 55 degrees, and the drink was a dandy. Highway construction turned off the tap, but the town built a lovely gazebo to mark the spot.

The springs around town sustained the community from the 1890s on: The Bath House, located at Heart Spring, where the Steamboat Health and Recreation Association is now, drew travelers, prospectors, and settlers from hundreds of miles. From the springs flowed business for hotels, restaurants, and other enterprises: Wounded veterans, victims of illnesses for which there were no cures, the wealthy from both coasts in search of a tonic for the stresses of industrial life, and health advocates who credited the hot water and minerals with restoring the body's natural chemical balances.

That same commerce killed another spring, the town's namesake, Steamboat Spring. Blasting for railroad construction in 1908 disturbed the bedrock and forever silenced the "chug." That spring and the town were named by three French trappers in the 1820s who had wandered up the Yampa River and heard a throaty, periodic chug. After months in the wilderness, they concluded that they'd hit a major river with paddle-wheel steamboats.

A long soak in the hot springs consoled the Frenchmen. Later, geologists explained that the chugging sound was created when the superheated water and steam hit an underground rock chamber. The flows were compressed until the buildup forced the steam out with a chug.

The Springs' Walk often starts at Iron Springs Park, located at 13th Street and Lincoln Avenue, next to the parking lot. This spring's water was considered a tonic for "ailments of body and will." At the turn of the century that meant everything from tuberculosis to depression, from arthritis to schizophrenia. An additional spritz of lemon juice was recommended, for the water tasted strongly of iron. As a point of fact, Soda Spring has a higher iron content, but generations swore by the Iron Spring cure.

Along the Springs' Walk, there is no bathing.

On the Yampa River's north bank is Sulphur Spring, which announces its name to your nose before it meets your eyes. The Utes believed the spring's scent signified powerful healing. European settlers found something tremendously appealing there. Enough people visited so that the spring was ringed with large stones embedded with tether rings for horses. Today the number of pawprints and hoofmarks found around the spring each morning indicate that wildlife has a singular preference for the pungent water.

Steamboat's early settlers were pleased with their progress, measured in sawmills, a flour mill, and two brickyards. The coming of the railroad in 1908 closed the brickyards, because the railroad could haul bricks into town more cheaply than the local yards could make them.

At Black Sulphur Spring, on the south side of the river, the water is inky black. The sulfur content is about the same as at Sulphur Spring, but it's got more of a witch's brew look. The original Steamboat Spring is located nearby and still has a geyserlike spurt. A few yards away are the Narcissus and Terrace Springs, as pretty as pearls in an oyster.

And then there's Lithia Spring. Lithia as in lithium, used in a mood-leveling drug and considered highly effective for manic depression. Modern chemical analysis found that other springs on the walk are higher in lithium, but stories have persisted for years about the chemical's effect on the population. Some said there was an Indian curse on the settlers that damned any who left the Yampa River Valley to great sadness. Others believed the waters were especially soothing because the pool's water is milky white. In the 1930s, a local advocate of Lithia's healing ways built stone columns at the spring's entrance and planned to sell bottled water with the label "Miraquelle." A local pharmacist says a glass or so of the water doesn't have enough lithium to make a difference in anybody's mood. Drinking the water along the Springs' Walk is prohibited for sanitary reasons.

Cave Spring has a different hot springs story. Elsewhere in the world there are similar caverns, where sulfur fumes are trapped. For ancient peoples these sites were often oracles or places where prophets were inspired by inhaling the fumes. Within Cave Spring, jets of hot water cut through the rough rock walls to form the cavern. And within that cavern lives a bacteria-algae descended from myceum, a life-form that dates back about 4 billion years. In other similar hot springs around the world, other bacteria-algae have evolved from myceum and have also remained simple primitive plants.

Hot Sulphur Springs Resort and Spa

P.O. Box 275
Hot Sulphur Springs 80451
(970) 725-3306
Open to the public; summer only; lodging; credit cards not accepted
Where: U.S. 40 between Granby and Steamboat Springs; the highway becomes Byers Avenue in Hot Sulphur Springs. On Byers at Park Street, located on the west side of town, turn north. Drive 1 block and turn west (left) onto Grand Street, cross the bridge over the Colorado River to the resort, which is on the north side of the river.

The Hot Sulphur Springs Resort and Spa is born anew. In 1996, a Denver renovator bought the tired and tattered property and transformed the pools, motel, spa, and 1840 cabin into one of Colorado's loveliest destination spas. More than twenty hot pools and private baths now tier the hillside and fill the spa. The temperatures range from 90 to 110 degrees Fahrenheit. The lobby, summer snack bar, and lockerooms are bright and clean. There are private vapor caves, a solarium pool, a summer swimming pool, and sunning areas linked by a maze of decks with nonslip surfaces. And the seventeen motel rooms are simple—no television or telephones in the rooms—but they're modern and comfortable. There's also a conference area.

It's amazing what vision and a few million dollars can do.

Hot Sulphur Springs reopened in 1997. At the moment a Ute holy man was blessing the springs' water, two eagles flew over. Since then, they've never had to advertise.

An outdoor soaking pool at Hot Sulphur Springs Resort and Spa.

"It's not all about money," says Charles Nash, the springs' magician who has converted several abandoned Denver Public Schools into condominiums. He's adamant that it's not a development, but a revival. "It's about relaxing and making people feel good."

However, he's put the springs on the market, including the 88 acres around the resort.

Located in a high mountain valley at 7,600 feet and flanked by the Continental Divide and the Gore Range, about seven springs flow from granite, gneiss, and sandstone. The resort and the town are cupped by the edge of the Arapahoe National Forest. The Colorado River runs past the resort, roaring from the head waters in the Never Summer Mountains all the way to the salt flats in Mexico.

The main spring is 125 degrees, but the pools vary from 90 to 110 degrees. The water isn't filtered, chemically treated, or recycled. The 200,000 gallons of fresh spring water that flow into the pools each day is just as it comes from the depths, bearing

Hot Sulphur Springs

tiny amounts sulfate, sodium, magnesium, fluoride, calcium, potassium, chloride, and traces of lithium and zinc. The spa's motto is "Soaking at it's Best."

The pleasant pools are scattered on a hillside near the Colorado river, about thirty minutes from Winter Park and about one hour from Steamboat Springs. Hot Sulphur Springs, at 7,600 feet, is a gateway to Rocky Mountain National Park and Grand Lake as well. And for railroad fans, there's a rail line across from the resort where Amtrak and freight cars pass with the whistles proudly sounding.

Hot Sulphur Springs has its own eclectic mix of guests: snowmobilers and orthodox Jews, hunters and Greek tourists, the usual après-ski or hiking crowds, county officials, and Tai Chi workshops. There's no smoking, alcohol, or pets allowed.

For those with children too young to enjoy hot pools, there's a swimming pool with a bathtub-warm temperature in the winter and a slightly balmy warmth in the summer where youngsters can frolic. There's also a kid's courtyard with shallow pools in a fenced enclosure, where supervised toddlers over six months of age can splash and cavort with like-minded kids.

At Hot Sulphur Springs today, every path leads to a hot pool. Many enjoy the Hillside Pool, surrounded by an 8-foot privacy fence and facing cat tails, a pond, the rail line, and a fairly quiet road. A cliff wall provides security on one side. The temperature ranges from 105 to 107. And, for a half hour or so, it's all yours.

That's how the Utes felt as the Europeans arrived and pushed tribes into smaller and smaller areas. The Utes had already fended off centuries of invasions by the Arapahoe and the Cheyenne. There's a story about a medicine man who couldn't stop the younger men from waging war on the rival tribes. When the young men didn't return from a raiding party, he built a campfire by the river. The earth absorbed his sadness and the fire's heat, creating the soothing hot springs.

As more settlers and soldiers came to the area, the Utes resorted to guerrilla war. Game was slaughtered, forests burned, and buildings set afire to scare the settlers out. All to no avail.

In 1863, William Byers, the flamboyant publisher of Denver's first newspaper, *The Rocky Mountain News*, bought the springs from a Sioux woman through a back-door deal. Byers envisioned an international resort of intellectuals, business tycoons, and prominent Americans. He built a summer home, the Willows, next to the hot springs pool.

His vision of "America's Switzerland" carried him through years in court over the title to the land, which he acquired from a Minnesota Sioux at a time when a U.S. treaty recognized the Utes as the rightful owners, according to *Island in the Rockies* by Robert Black III. Byers won, but complained bitterly about the court costs. His dream resort never fully materialized because the railroad didn't arrive until 1928 and winter travel to the remote valley was often impossible.

Ever the optimist, Byers built a race track, a large hotel, a covered swimming pool and offered other amenities. The stagecoach and later the railroad dropped off passengers from the East Coast for a week of recuperation in the invigorating mountain air and rejuvenation in the springs. Before rail service, pioneers traveled from as far as the other side of Berthoud Pass to visit the baths, even though in the early years when guests had to ford the river to reach the springs.

Hot Sulphur Springs did afford Byers a good view on every major act in the state's early settlement—trapping, gold mining, ambitious railroad projects, forest clear cuts, and homesteading—as the boom and bust series played out in the Middle Park Valley surrounding Hot Sulphur Springs.

Territorial Governor William Gilpin, removed from office in 1862, and his successor, Territorial Governor John Evans, were friends of Byers and wanted the Middle Park area around Hot Sulphur Springs settled. "The Utes Must Go" was their campaign theme. Evans was ousted for his part in a 1864 Sand Creek Massacre of Cheyenne and Arapahoe, mostly women and children.

The western author Zane Gray rented a cabin nearby, and John Wesley Powell practiced running the Colorado River's rapids near town in wooden boats for his expedition down the Grand Canyon.

The Moffat Tunnel punched through the Continental Divide in 1928, in part, to reach the springs. David Moffat, railroad pioneer, spent $10 million of his own money to build a line west to Utah and the Pacific. Moffat had made his fortune by buying mines and building rail lines to the gold and silver fields in Aspen, Creede, Leadville, and Cripple Creek. Moffat was president of the Denver and Rio Grande until the board refused in 1902 to take on the westward line. He died in 1911. The rails eventually reached Craig, but never Utah. Amtrak still uses Moffat's namesake tunnel to reach the Winter Park Resort, but there's no longer a stop at Hot Sulphur Springs.

At night, the lodge roof is outlined in green neon and pool walkways are marked with movie-seating lights. At the Ute pool, a grotto with a flagstone edge where the water tumbles down from a rock chute in a cascade that out pours any shower, the splash blots out other sounds. Two centuries of conquest, settlement, and tourism dissolve. The springs murmur a transcendent welcome.

Eldorado Springs

294 Artesian Drive
Eldorado Springs 80015
(303) 499-1316

Open to the public; summer hours only; credit cards not accepted
Where: From Boulder, take Colorado 93 south to Colorado 170.
From west 6th Avenue in Denver, drive west to Golden and turn
north onto Colorado 93. Take Colorado 93 north past Rocky Flats
to Colorado 170. Turn west and follow Eldorado Springs Drive up
into the foothills for about 3 miles. Drive through the town of
Eldorado Springs. The pool complex is on the right side of the
road at the west end of town.

T he water isn't hot here. It flows from a natural artesian spring
and is only 76 degrees.

The Eldorado Springs pool has been open every summer since
1904. The pool stretches out in a narrow canyon where mountaineers scale the heights, hikers wander for miles, spring-water
fans fill up for twenty-five cents a jug, railroad buffs walk the abandoned Moffat line, and swimmers frolic in the cool water during
the summer months.

Once a winter camp for Indians, including the Colorado Utes,
the springs later became a mystic spot for turn-of-the-century spiritualists who worshipped its purity and natural origins. Later,
Eldorado Springs was the honeymoon roost for Dwight and Mamie
Eisenhower. Today, Eldorado Springs's narrow steep canyon has
evolved into a climbing mecca for mountaineers training to tackle
the major peaks of the world. On a 90-degree day the pool is teem-
ing with people. When the temperatures drop below 70 it gets
pretty quiet. Eldorado Springs loyalists love it here, because the
water temperature keeps the crowds down.

The Coney Island of Colorado—Eldorado Springs in 1907. (Photograph courtesy Colorado Historical Society)

An artesian spring occurs where water seeps into cracks above the spring's outlet and the water flows without pumping because of the pressure from above. Oil exploration or well building sometimes creates artesian springs when drilling reaches naturally formed underground chambers where water flows through geologic faults. Eldorado Springs has both natural springs and several artesian wells.

The pool and resort are located at the entrance to Eldorado Springs State Park. In the park, the vertical walls that climbers call the Bastille, Wind Tower, and The Naked Edge are dotted with mountaineers. On almost any day of the year, from the road into the canyon dozens of climbers are visible on the cliffs above. Free climbers scrambling without ropes, climbers roped together in twos and threes and fours, solo climbers scaling the heights, and beginning climbers practicing on the lower reaches all leave trails of chalk on the handholds in the rock.

The road through the town of Eldorado Springs isn't paved. The potholes qualify as kiddie pools, and some stretch 6 and 7 feet across the dirt track. The populace likes the road that way—it slows down the perpetual traffic.

Front Range Area

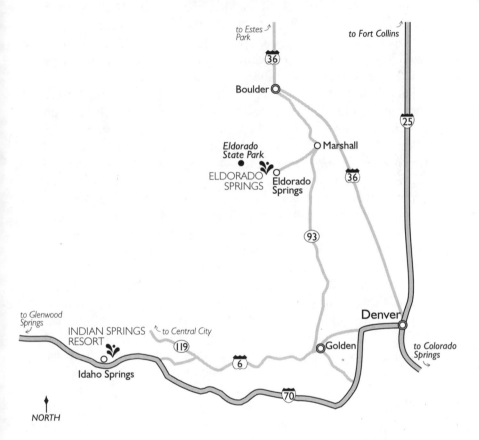

to Estes Park

to Fort Collins

36

Boulder

25

Eldorado State Park

Marshall

ELDORADO SPRINGS

Eldorado Springs

36

93

to Glenwood Springs

Denver

INDIAN SPRINGS RESORT

to Central City

119

Golden

to Colorado Springs

6

Idaho Springs

70

NORTH

The Utes named the narrow canyon for the yellow-and-orange-lichen–tinged cliff walls. The Ute term was translated into Spanish as *El Dorado*, or "the gilded one." In 1860, wagon train leader Charles Barber chanced on the spot, ran the Indians off, and set up a mining and logging operation. Within forty years Barber had clear-cut the canyon, and his attempt to build a narrow-gauge rail line to haul out the timber had cleaned him out financially.

The spiritualists came next, searching for a terrestrial link to the spirit world and convinced that those in the next world could travel the waterway. Frank Fowler, who bought the property in 1904 to create the Moffat Lakes Resort, saw a good business prospect in the springs rather than messages from beyond. He and three partners put in a swimming pool and eight sets of "crazy stairs" that zigzagged 1,350 feet up the cliffs. The swimming pool was the only one in Colorado until after World War I. People hiked in high boots, full suits, or long dresses. For swimming, the women wore tennis shoes, black stockings, belts, and bloomers—twice as many clothes for bathing as for walking.

The famed Ivy Baldwin arrived in 1907. Called "The Human Fly," Baldwin strung a 3/8-inch-thick wire across the 630-foot-wide canyon and made eighty-nine successful transits 582 feet above the creek. The man who made ladies swoon with fright and strong men gasp died of natural causes in his own bed at age eighty-two in 1953. He walked the high wire until 1948.

Touted as the "Coney Island of Colorado," where there were cool nights with no mosquitoes or dust, Eldorado Springs was a mecca during the summer for refugees from city heat and congestion. By 1905, the Denver and Interurban Electric Line carried up to two thousand people a weekend to Eldorado Springs. In 1908 a three-story hotel opened that hosted Mary Pickford, Jack Dempsey, and Damon Runyon before it burned down in 1939. In the 1940s the Glenn Miller Orchestra headlined at the Eldorado ballroom, and another generation of young couples started married life, like the Eisenhowers, by casting dreams in the stars above the canyon.

Kevin Sipple, Doug Larson, and Jeremy Martin bought the springs in 1983, mostly for the bottled-water business, Eldorado

Artesian Springs. Kevin is chairman of the board, vice president of marketing, the town's water superintendent, water-plant operator, and head of ditch construction. In 1996, at the Sixth International Festival of the Water Toaster's Tap, Eldorado Artesian Springs water placed third in the best-tasting municipal water category, out of a field of seventy-nine contestants from around the world.

The bottling plant is located in the resort's old ballroom and home-delivers about twelve hundred bottles a day. Kevin says the water is so clean that it doesn't have to be purified, and the natural carbonation keeps it bacteria-free. There's also a faucet on the grounds for filling jugs—twenty-five cents each on the honor system.

There's a building around the main spring, but smaller springs are located outside, near the river. Even when temperatures plunge below zero the water still flows, and the grass stays green year-round—evidence of an eternal spring within each seemingly eternal winter.

Indian Springs Resort

302 Soda Creek Road
P.O. Box 1990
Idaho Springs 80452
(303) 989-6666
www.indianspringsresort.com
Open to the public; lodging; credit cards accepted
Where: From Denver, take Interstate 70 west to Exit 241, the first Idaho Springs turnoff. Stay on the Exit road, which becomes Colorado Boulevard going west through town. At Miner Street, turn left. At the Colorado Boulevard–Miner Street intersection is the town information center, which creates a **Y** in the road. Take Miner Street to Soda Creek Road and turn left (south). Go under the highway overpass—the resort is on the left. See map, page 23.

The swimming pool is lovely and the thermal caves are a step into the geologic past, but no other hot springs gives you mud. It's Club Mud, to be exact. Not flashy, just a room near the swimming pool with a white-tiled vat of mud, a heat blower to hasten the drying process, and a shower. The walls and ceiling are decorated with mud handprints, names written with mud, quick sketches in mud, and a few cartoons in the mud medium. Club Mud's cleaning regime removes the pictographs and new mud masterpieces take their place.

People from the pool line up on the other side of the window at Club Mud to watch the show. There's a tradition among the mud people to provide a show. When the mud dries, every move sends up a billow of dust. A pat on the back is like shaking a dusty rug. Clapping hands creates a dust storm. Tap dancing summons a dust devil. No other Colorado hot springs offers mud rooms—they are unique to Indian Springs, an added attraction to the resort's hot tubs and pools.

The swimming pool at Indian Springs Resort.

The resort is hard to miss from Interstate 70—a large billboard flashes Indian Hot Springs at motorists with large silver, pink, and blue sequins. It's a luxurious stop on the way home from skiing, biking, or camping in the mountains, or a thirty-minute drive from the Denver area for an afternoon's or evening's repose.

Housed in a vintage hotel, the springs are pleasantly Old World. The men's and the women's caves, located in geothermal tunnels, are separated. In the tradition of European spas, no clothing is allowed.

The women's caves are a huge subterranean honeycomb with individual cells off the main tunnel. The lighting in places is good enough to read, but most ladies just soak in the hot tubs. The ground-level thermal tubs, encased in the marbleized agate of the springs' own mineral deposits, vary in width and length. Some accommodate three soakers, others only one. In the quiet, there is a calm. The tunnel cuts through rock, and there's the security that comes with being cradled within the earth. Internal clocks slow down. The mind's obsessive turning loosens a bit. The water is warmer than skin—104 to 112 degrees—and, with closed eyes, the line between the two melts.

In the past two hundred years, Indian Springs itself hasn't seen much rest. By 1867 gold mining was taking off in Clear Creek Canyon, across the river, and hundreds of miners had moved to town. Gold dust and nuggets were the standard currency, and sales of "tangle-foot," a potent home brew, were brisk. The gold rush pushed the Utes and the Arapahoe out of the area. The springs had been on the dividing line between their territories, and both tribes used the caves and hot pools peaceably for decades.

George A. Jackson, who discovered the first placer gold in Colorado, chanced on the Soda springs while exploring Clear Creek. He spotted a dense mist rising above Soda Creek on January 1, 1859, and wrote in his diary: "Killed a mountain lion today. Made about eight miles and camped at warm springs near mouth of small creek. Snow all gone around springs."

Jackson returned in later years and saw a large geyser that eventually sank, leaving a legacy of small springs. But more important, he was the first to find a gold nugget and gold dust in the creek. At first, the town was "Jackson's Diggins." The name shifted to "Sacramento Flats," a name favored by the California gold miners in the area. Finally, "Idaho" was selected by consensus, although the name had no particular local significance. "Springs" was added to honor the enduring resource.

Gold miners created the subterranean tunnels and were disappointed to find nothing but hot water. In 1863, Dr. C. M. Cummings saw the possibilities and built a bathhouse for the "hot water mine." Harrison Montague bought the property in 1866, built the Ocean Bath House out of stone and wood, added a hotel, and declared the spot the "Saratoga of the Rocky Mountains," after a famous spa in New York.

A group of investors paid $76,000 for the resort in 1902, spent $35,000 on extending the tunnels, dug the baths, renovated the hotel, and connected other hot springs to swimming pools. Unfortunately, the stockholders' resources fell short of the owners' enthusiasm for more improvements. So in 1911 Indian Springs was sold to another investment company. Since then, more owners and managers have come and gone, but the resort has grown to encompass approximately eighty rooms in the main lodge and two modern additions. The hot springs and the mountain setting resort have drawn the likes of Frank and Jesse James, Walt Whitman, assorted Vanderbilts and Roosevelts, and Sarah Bernhardt.

James Maxwell, Indian Springs' current owner, also owns the nearby Argo Gold Mill, which offers daily tours through the shafts, processing area, and waste pits. The mill is over one hundred years old, and the process for extracting gold from the ore hasn't changed much in a century. If the weather's right and you're so inclined, pan for gold. The lucky few can keep any gleaming flakes found in their pans.

Radium Hot Springs

In Grand County, in the state's Radium Wildlife Area
No charge; clothing optional; primitive location
Where: Park at the Mugrage Campground before Radium, walk to
the toilets, and from there cross the street and head up the trail by
the telephone switcher box. The trails are many and interlace. Just
head toward the river for about a mile and, when you reach the
River Rim Trail, go right for 1/4 mile. Look for the short stretch of
sheer rock canyon wall on the river, and the hot spring is at the
base of the geological outcropping's midway point. Footprints and
flattened plants mark the trail that drops down about 50 feet.

Keep this a secret. Radium Hot Springs isn't on any of the maps.
And unless you've spotted it by floating by on a raft or someone's given you great directions, it's nearly impossible to find. Once
you find it, you'll realize that dozens of foot paths and four-wheel-
drive vehicle trails will take you there, but only in a hither and
thither way.

Located a mile or so upstream on the Colorado River from the
on-the-edge of ghosthood town of Radium, is the riverside hot
pot rimmed with rocks. The spot is about 50 vertical feet down
from a trail along a rocky rim. Another fairly easy route in is to
follow the foot trail that starts near the parking lot at the Radium
Wildlife Area boat ramp. The only landmark, other than an occasional glimpse of the pool from the trail, is that the springs are
located in an volcanic outcropping that also left sheer and dark
cliffs on each side of the river. The house-height rock walls mark
the spot. The spot, for the global-positioning-system-empowered
as of January 1, 2000, was north 39-57-35, west 106-32-27.

The pool, large enough for twenty or so, draws boaters, the
folks that make the Vail and Aspen resorts run by washing dishes,
waiting tables, and selling lift tickets, an occasional exuberant

Radium Hot Springs

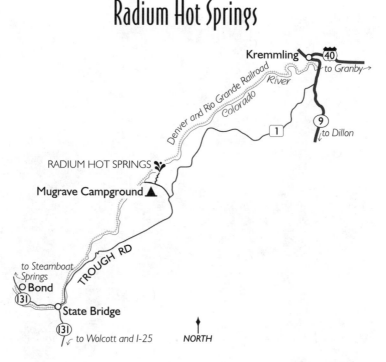

Radium Hot Springs awaits soakers.

hunting party, and long-time locals. Visitors in fall or spring may have the pleasure of solo dipping.

When soaking in the rock enclave, positioning near the springs' underwater outflows is everything. The pool temperatures run in the 90s, depending on how well the outer rock edge has been packed with sand to prevent seepage. The flows, which are tiny, trickle from half a dozen springs at the site and are in the low 100s. So, soaking on a summer or fall day is delightful, but it's not a place people linger long in winter after the sun has gone down.

The town of Radium was named in 1906 by Harry Porter who opened a mine that contained small amounts of radium. Not to worry. Colorado soil frequently contains low levels of radioactivity, yet the state's cancer rate isn't high.

But along the rim side trail from the Radium boat dock and where the Mugrage Campground Trail hits the rim, there are a half dozen splendid camping spots with rock fire rings and extraordinary views of the river, the rolling hills, and the peaks.

Across the river from the pool are the Denver and Rio Grande Western railroad tracks. A few, long freight trains pass everyday and many more at night. The engineer and crews are obliging— they'll blow the whistle when soakers wave. Sometimes an au natural crowd will provoke a couple short bursts. And rafters, canoers, kayakers, and other floaters stop by to warm up before heading down to the traditional takeout point at State Bridge.

Ah, State Bridge, an enclave of throwbacks to the 1960s and 1970s. River runners, hippies, the drivers of classic old Fords, VW bugs, and Chevies, and rock-and-roll fiends. There's a few cabins, a few boat ramps, a bar, and restaurant with live music every summer weekend and a big dance floor on the patio. There aren't even any full time residents to complain about the noise. It's a town that industrial tourism forgot. In 1941, a guidebook described it as "a cluster of weathered buildings." Blessedly, it hasn't changed much.

Please keep Radium Hot Springs the way you find it. I tell you about it in hopes caring soakers will treasure the spring by the river and leave it better than they found it. A visit in late fall of 1999 found broken glass at the bottom of the pool, dog waste ringing the bathing area, and cigarette butts scattered in the brush, shallows, and rock ledges. You can either make it better or worse. Has the hot spring ethic survived? Will people protect a spot of beauty and delight or will they pursue their own selfish desires without concern for the negative impact on other soakers?

You will decide.

Yampah Spa and Vapor Caves

709 East 6th Avenue
Glenwood Springs 81601
(970) 945-0667
Open to the public; credit cards accepted
Where: From Interstate 70 through Glenwood Springs, take Exit 116. From the exit ramp, turn north (south will put you back on Interstate 70) and drive 1 block to the stoplight and an intersection. The Village Inn is on the left—west. Turn right—east—onto 6th Street. Drive past Grand Avenue and the "big" pool at the Glenwood Springs Lodge and Pool. As the road narrows, turn left into Yampah's parking lot. See map, page 41.

The silence and perpetual darkness set the vapor caves at the Yampah Spa apart from Colorado's other hot springs. The cement-lined tunnel down the stairs leads bathers to a maze of steamy chambers, some cool and some hot. Only whispers and a primeval dripping sound break the silence. The quiet is not so much the absence of noise as it is the presence of silence.

"Hygienic Hades" read the headline from the 1894 *Harper's Weekly* story illustrated with a woodcut of wounded men reclining in the caves. "Springs of water hot from the fires below . . ." emit sulfurous fumes with curative powers over lead-poisoned miners from Cripple Creek and nicotine-ridden smokers, wrote William A. Rogers.

The Yampah Spa has the only known natural vapor caves in North America. Vapor caves occur when small hot springs flow through hollow underground chambers, coating the walls, ceiling, and floor with water, steam, and heat.

At Yampah there are no pools or cooling baths beyond the showers upstairs. Those who spend all day in the caves use the

An early vapor bathhouse in Glenwood. (Photograph courtesy Colorado Historical Society)

cold shower in the caves and slip into the cooling rooms to control body temperature. Each chamber has elevated marble slabs dating back to 1893 for reclining and sitting. Lying in the dark gloom, this bather felt like ancient royalty laid out for permanent rest. Artificial lighting highlights the caverns stretching outward from each cave, thus mitigating the closed-in feeling.

The Utes used the caves for ceremonies, healing, and respites from winter's cold and the aches of aging. Each Memorial Day, contemporary Utes return to Glenwood for an intertribal conference and join others in the caves seeking spiritual and physical purification.

In 1879, Glenwood Springs' founder, Isaac Cooper, was toiling in the Leadville mines. The Civil War had stolen his youth and his health. When he heard the Utes extol the healing power of the hot springs and vapor caves at the confluence of two rivers, the Colorado and the Crystal, he set off with a few similarly desperate miners in the midst of winter on a 60-mile trek over the Continental Divide to the Glenwood area. Once there, he never left.

An entrepreneur opened the vapor caves to the public within a few years of the town's founding. "One of the most singular things that use of the waters effects is the certain bringing back to bald heads of full heads of hair and this is done inside of three months by rubbing with the water, once daily. This is a literal fact," wrote M. L. DeCoursey in 1884. He managed the pools.

The Yampah Spa and Vapor Caves are part of a geological network of vapor caves and hot springs along the Colorado River. Some of the springs were destroyed by construction when Interstate 70 was widened. Others went when the river's channel was changed. On the other side of the river from the spa, additional vapor caves are used periodically by transient men during the winter.

The spa and caves were first developed in the modest Victorian era, and the caves were divided for male and female bathers. Separation of the sexes continued until the late 1980s. Even today, elderly bathers from other states occasionally arrive without bathing suits, expecting a wall to protect their modesty. Fortunately, they usually have a suit in the car and can then indulge in the vapor caves, which were renovated in 1990.

Within the caves, the 125-degree spring water is channeled along the sides of each chamber to create a natural steam bath. Drains collect the still too-hot-to-touch water and reroute it under the floor to raise the temperature further. Upstairs are a solarium, massage rooms, hot tubs, lockers, showers, and a spa. The scent is of fresh water and sulfur. (However, this faithful hot springs surveyor didn't smell much of anything.)

The Yampah Spa and Vapor Caves, mindful of the sensitive noses and tastes of youngsters, allows families to walk around the subterranean steam bath before buying tickets. Few children opt to stay, but one wonders whether the enormous Glenwood Springs pool next door influences the decisions more than the sulfur does.

Within the dimly lit and womblike chambers, time slows and stops. Given enough time and an occasional splash of cold water, the steam and heat melt away worries and real-world woes. The mind wanders. Within the vapor clouds, visual distractions vanish. And when it's time to leave, the walk upstairs is like waking up energized from a good, deep sleep. There's a sense of having returned far better for the trip.

Glenwood Springs Hot Springs, Lodge, and Pool

401 North River Street
P.O. Box 308
Glenwood Springs 81602
(970) 945-6571
www.hotspringspool.com
Open to the public; lodging; credit cards accepted
Where: From Interstate 70 through Glenwood Springs, take Exit 116. From the exit ramp, turn north (south will put you back on Interstate 70) and drive 1 block to the stoplight and an intersection. The Village Inn is on the left—west. Turn right—east—onto 6th Street. Drive past Grand Avenue and the Hotel Colorado. Turn right at the edge of the pool grounds and into the parking lot. See map, page 41.

This is the big one. The Glenwood Hot Springs Pool is so big that there's room for scuba divers, lap swimming, kids with rafts and balls, parents teaching youngsters to swim, lovers lost in the mist, arthritis sufferers seeking relief, and lone blissed-out bathers. All at the same time, and without bumping into one another.

Put simply, this pool is the largest outdoor hot springs facility in the United States. The hot springs' flow is so great that it fills the 2-block-long pool and heats the newly renovated lodge.

You can visit the spring, contained in a stone-encased pool behind a chain-link fence. The pale blue-green pond looks like a Caribbean lagoon except for the steam that pours off even on the hottest days. The flow is 3.5 million gallons a day. The big pool, 405 feet long and 100 feet wide at its widest point, holds more than 1 million gallons of water at about 90 degrees. The small soaking pool, 100 feet wide, brews 91,000 gallons of water at 104 degrees.

There's more than enough room for everyone at the Glenwood Hot Springs Pool.

Glenwood Springs

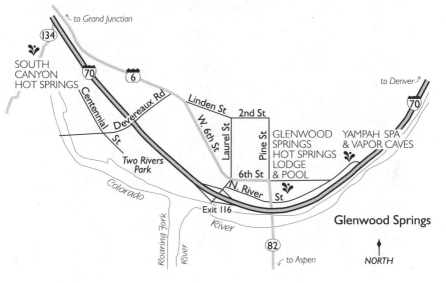

Local swimmers rack up thousands of miles a year. People come from miles around for the annual New Year's Eve splash. There's no drinking allowed at the pool—not even on New Year's Eve. Landlocked underwater explorers learn to scuba dive in the deep end. Uncounted thousands of children have learned to swim here, aided by the extra buoyancy of the mineral-laden waters. Newlyweds, lovers, and soon-to-be adults have charted their futures by looking up through the wafting steam to the myriad stars above. "The pool is many things to many people," says Kjell Mitchell, the pool's manager. "We're proud of that tradition."

Older people slip silently into the toasty warm waters of the shallow pool from 9:00 A.M. on. Some seniors groups have gathered together here for years, seeking comfort from aches and pains while enjoying the company. Thus, Glenwood Hot Springs lore is full of stories about people who moved to town nearly crippled, spent months in the therapy pool, and now either work at the lodge or hold other jobs in town. These days, the over-recreated take refuge in the hot pool to ease out the kinks of steep hikes, long days on the slopes, tough rock climbs, and challenging bike rides. And long before it was fashionable, there was a separate kiddie pool for toddlers.

At one time, a mineral cocktail from another spring on the premises was considered a tonic or a cure. Today there's a drinking-water spring with large doses of sodium chloride, sulfate of potassium, sulfate of lime, bicarbonate of lime, and magnesia. Vitamin pills and bottled water taste better.

Goldie Hawn, John Denver, Kurt Russell, and the cast of stars from Aspen's Planet Hollywood club appear from time to time—usually not during the crowded summer months. Gangster Al Capone once luxuriated unnoticed in the tendrils of mist. "Our tradition has always been to respect the privacy of our bathers," says Kjell, deflecting queries about other luminaries.

When the town's founder, Civil War veteran Isaac Cooper, obtained the big spring after the Utes were exiled in 1881, the temperature was 124 degrees and the flow was 3 million gallons a day. The world has changed, but not the spring.

Cooper, who crossed the mountains from Leadville in the dead of winter after hearing about the springs, promptly named the town-to-be for his home in Glenwood, Iowa. Within a few years, Cooper's efforts put the Glenwood stagecoach stop on the map as a destination resort. Health and hilarity were bywords as the hot springs attracted the wealthy, the famous, and the ailing.

New settlers to the area claimed smaller springs along the river, scooped out pools, and used pine boughs to make shelters. Aspen's silver mines mandated a rail line through Glenwood, and when the first Colorado Midland train arrived in 1887, the trip was heralded by 3,500 bonfires, set and tended by ecstatic locals.

The sandstone and terra-cotta lodge opened in 1890 with one bathhouse converted into a casino—for gentlemen only. The big pool was completed the next year. Even a whisper about public bathing sent Victorian ladies into a mass swoon. The first-floor rooms next to the pool each included a private indoor sunken tub. (Offices replaced the tubs during the early 1990s renovation.)

The Colorado Hotel accepted guests three years later. Built with English money, the hotel offered the sophisticated comforts considered essential to a resort catering to millionaires who arrived in private railroad cars. Diamond Jim Brady, Doc Holliday, and Buffalo Bill Cody provided color at the poker table and the pools. Presidents Theodore Roosevelt and William Taft visited during their tenures in office, soaking in the misty pools and drinking quarts of the mineral-laden water.

In the early 1940s the pool grounds included a sandy beach and striped cabanas. The pool and hotel were drafted by the navy in World War II: The hotel became a hospital and the pool a rehabilitation center. In 1956, twenty-two Glenwood Springs businessmen bought the property and retain ownership today. Mitchell's father was one of the buyers.

Although 75 percent of the resort's customers come from Denver, the area has a cornucopia of visitor attractions year-round: the Glenwood Canyon bike path; dozens of hikes for day-trippers; the Aspen, Sunlight, and Vail ski areas, all within an hour's drive; horseback riding; rafting; rock climbing; hunting; fishing; day-long cattle drives; and the magic kingdom of Aspen itself. Glenwood is one of the few tourist destinations in Colorado served by trains from Denver.

And then there's Agnes.

Agnes the ghost. Since the bathhouse was built in 1890, doors have been slamming and windows opening or closing when no one is around. There are footsteps in empty halls and toilets flushing in unoccupied rooms. The staff today credits Agnes. No one knows who Agnes was or why she's remained in the building. Kjell Mitchell, a discreet host and modern manager, sighs when asked about Agnes and offers no insights. "I've never heard anyone say they knew who she was," says Kjell, who grew up around the pool hearing Agnes stories.

Agnes, according to pool lore, is more active at night, although she rarely actually appears. Bathers report seeing the ghost of an old woman. In the coffee shop, pots of coffee have vanished.

If you happen to see Agnes, say hello for me.

South Canyon

South Canyon Creek Road
Glenwood Springs

An ever-evolving series of hillside pools and hot pots on county-owned land; no services; primitive setting

Where: Heading west on Interstate 70, about five miles from Glenwood Springs, take exit 111, South Canyon. The road winds around and heads south up County Road 134, the South Canyon Creek Road. From where the road crosses the Colorado River, drive half a mile and pull off to the right into a small turnout. On the right of the turnout and along the edge is a 1/4-mile path that leads down through trees, over a creek, and up a hillside to the pools.

South Canyon qualifies as a wild spring by virtue of its location near the Garfield County dump, west of Glenwood Springs, and the design, which seems to change several times a year.

On a good day, the water is clear, the surrounding natural grasses are green, and it's a wonderful wildland spring. Carpet samples soften the sitting on the pools' edges, and there's not a speck of trash to be seen. On a bad day, which was six months earlier in 1999, the several hillside hot pots were muddy and shallow, the area was littered with broken glass, cigarette butts, and trash, and one pool had been undammed and destroyed.

Let the hot springs cards fall where they may. South Canyon is always an adventure.

On that second summer visit in 1999, white plastic piping funneled the water between the deep lagoons of two large pools. Rocks were arranged for small group conversations. And the waters were blessedly uninhabited although a steady traffic of garbage trucks and loaded pickups paraded past to the county dump.

The land is owned by Garfield County, and there's a long saga of episodic enforcement of the "no bathing, no nudity, no dope

South Canyon spiffed up by unofficial caretakers.

smoking, and no drinking" rules. While the current mode seems
to be live and let live, complaints could arouse a new wave of visits from the sheriff's patrol.

Finding the springs is tricky, but once you're there it's a "how
did I miss it?" kind of place. It's above the level of the road, across
the stream and up a winding goat path. Once you're there, you're
there. But the pools and springs aren't readily visible until you're
standing next to the water.

The pools offer a 180-degree view that includes the rocky hillside, the fire scorched Storm King Mountain to the north, South
Canyon Creek Valley, and the land-fill entrance. Although housing
developments have cropped up in nearly every valley in the area,
the spring's location near a dump may protect its "viewshed" for
the near future.

Glenwood Springs is the street corner for resort country. The
highway to Aspen juts off in one direction and the highway to Vail
runs toward the east. It's a dose of reality between the two glitter
gulches. There's never been a rumor about anyone famous bathing

at South Canyon. But the springs provided a front row seat for one of the deadliest forest fires of the 1900s—the Storm King in 1994. Looking north from the springs, the farthest ridge top was still black two years after the blaze that consumed 2,100 acres and killed fourteen firefighters.

In the next decade the hillsides will regrow vegetation and the scars will fade as soakers at South Canyon will see. The hot pots at South Canyon host a lively crowd. People who haven't visited in ten and twenty years, who reconnoitered the site by memory, the local population of transients who frequent thermal caves on the other side of town and the big pool's outflows, and dozens of new soakers ecstatic about the adventure. Some go natural, abandoning clothes on the rocks. Others use the trees as a changing chamber. From the improvements and the shipshape conditions found on a third trip in 1999, it appears the springs have a new patron or two, devoted to their upkeep.

The flows are about 118 degrees, but the pools run closer to 106 degrees. South Canyon earned the name "Hippie Dip" in the 1960s when wildly painted VW buses and battered cars clogged the road and skinny dippers frolicked in the pools. The number of visitors tapered off, blessedly for the county, which also tried to bulldoze and destroy the pools. Today, few days pass without a few soakers although the county commissioners periodically take up South Canyon as a topic because of drunkenness, fights, and nudity at the pools.

The pools at South Canyon can be a nice respite from a busy day spent on the river, climbing, mountain biking along Glenwood Canyon's bike path, playing cowboy at a mock daylong cattle drive, floating the river, or exploring the back roads that crisscross the hills. The area also has numerous caves, including the recently reopened Fairy Caves; miles of caverns and passages; and rare mineral formations such as cave bacon, soda straws, and crystalline wing-like formations created nine million years ago by the Colorado River.

Indeed, the geological whimsy that created the maze of grottoes and caves is best contemplated from that other phenomenon of geological wit—a hot springs.

Penny Hot Springs

On Colorado 133 between Carbondale and Marble
No charge; clothing optional; primitive
Where: From Glenwood Springs, take Colorado 82 south to Carbondale. From Carbondale, take Colorado 133 south toward Redstone and Marble. About 15 miles south of Carbondale—before Redstone—is a turnout on the left (east). At the south end of the well-used turnout is a very small "C.R. 11" sign. The Crystal River flows next to Colorado 133 at this point, and the hot springs are downhill from the turnout and on the edge of the river.

Penny Hot Springs is thrice a surprise. That the steamy natural pool in the Crystal River between Carbondale and Redstone survived a late 1980s war between skinny-dippers and a rancher across the river is one surprise. The second surprise is that the rocky beach and the ponds are pristine—conscientious bathers remove bottles, dirty diapers, cans, film boxes, paper, and other debris. At Penny, the unwritten ethic is that each set of bathers leaves the place cleaner than they found it.

And the third surprise is that the shape, size, and configurations of the soaking pools constantly change, sometimes overnight. As with most "free" undeveloped springs, each bather adjusts the rocks to form a personally tailored pool.

Most days, Penny is a roadside delight. Named after an early rancher and tucked down a dirt trail 15 feet from a highway

Penny Hot Springs

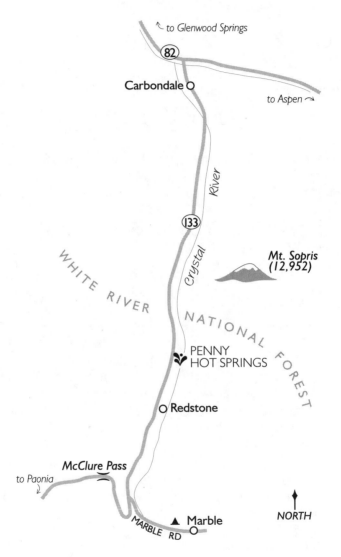

to Glenwood Springs

82

Carbondale O

to Aspen

River

133

Crystal

Mt. Sopris
(12,952)

WHITE RIVER

NATIONAL FOREST

PENNY
HOT SPRINGS

O Redstone

McClure Pass

to Paonia

▲ Marble
O

MARBLE RD

NORTH

turnout, the springs are located on a highway easement now owned by Pitkin County. In the winter, rising steam and densely packed cars mark the spot. A small county road sign (CR 11) at the turnoff helps during the rest of the year.

In the spring, snowmelt from the mountains floods over the springs. Late-summer flows in drought years drains the pool. And early-spring runoff turns the Crystal River's water toffee brown.

The Colorado Geological Survey puts the springs' temperature at about 130 degrees. Seeps are scattered along the riverbank. The hot water rises, which means the bathing pools may have icy cold river-water bottoms. The result is a ritual movement akin to a hen settling on a large clutch of eggs. Determined bathers stand in place, move in circles, and gradually lower themselves into a position of comfort between the heat of the thermals and the cold of the river. Frequent agitation of the water is usually required.

This explains the regular reconfiguration of the rocks and the pools as bather-engineers strive for the perfect mix for hot springs bliss. Utes, miners, cowboys, hippies, and skiers have found delight on the banks of the Crystal for over a century. In the late 1980s, a truck full of boulders and charges of trespassing and indecent exposure closed the area. Local hot springs folk hero Roy Rickus, who wore only a turban to bathe in the springs, led the local spring loyalists against a neighboring rancher who didn't like nude bathing in view of his riverside pasture. Roy lost a claim in state water court to become the springs' trustee but was acquitted of indecent exposure in the local court.

Perhaps Roy prevailed in a higher court—the long term. The load of boulders slowly shifted, the spring returned, and his guardianship prevails.

Fans honk as they drive by the turnout. Beware of sudden spring floods that cascade over Penny for a month at a time. In heavy-snow years with a stretch of hot spring days, the water level can jump a foot in an hour, enough warning for even the most relaxed bather.

A bather-engineered pool at Penny Hot Springs.

Conundrum Hot Springs

Maroon Bells–Snowmass Wilderness Area
White River National Forest
No charge; clothing optional; primitive wilderness location
Where: From Aspen, take Colorado 82 northwest about 1/4-mile,
turn left at Maroon Creek Road (FS 102) and take the immediate
left to Castle Creek Road. Drive for 5 miles and turn right onto
Conundrum Road. Drive 1.1 miles to the Conundrum Creek
Trailhead parking lot. Avoid parking elsewhere—adjacent private
landowners have vehicles towed. To get to the spring, it's a 9-mile
hike one way, with a 2,700-foot elevation gain to 11,200 feet.
USGS map: Hayden Peak, Maroon Bells.

The conundrum about Conundrum. It's remote. A tough nine-
mile hike *each way*. A 2,700-foot elevation gain to 11,200 feet.
And the idyllic site is crowded by up to four hundred people on a
summer weekend.

The once-fair spot is overrun, overused, and abused. The U.S.
Forest Service will be testing the spring water and the creek in the
years ahead for human and canine waste. If the tests show conta-
mination, the springs will be closed to the public.

To omit mention of Conundrum Hot Springs in a guidebook is an
act of kindness, and conservation. Or is leaving it out a cop-out? A
bogus high-minded excuse born of reluctance to make the strenuous
expedition? Those were my thoughts in 1999 when I checked on
Conundrum's well-being. When I tried to visit in the spring a few
years earlier, the snow and cold kept the spot at 11,200 feet locked.
The snow kept the trail to Conundrum closed into July. But by August,
the trailhead parking lot and the two long meadows along the road
were packed with cars.

Enchantment at Conundrum Hot Springs.

And in mid-September, the desire to protect one of the last best places lost out to twenty years of journalistic credo to write from experience, not second- and third-hand accounts. Rains and snow postponed the trip a day and compressed what was meant to be an overnight adventure into a single day.

The maps are deceptive. The first 3 miles are a fool's trap. The illusion of an easy day hike was bolstered by locals' claims that the trip's a snap. That's pure fantasy, unless you work out at high altitudes for two hours a day. The trek is a thigh-killing, blood-blistering, air-gasping forced march. Some of Colorado's 14,000-foot peaks are easier to climb.

But at trail's end, Conundrum Hot Springs smiles from a willow marsh, coyly promising a warmwater embrace that will resolve any hesitations about visiting. Located at the edge of the tree line and fringed by stocky brush, the springs are a wonderment. Above are towering peaks, avalanche chutes, mountainsides of broken slate, and an azure sky that's rarely seen. The setting exclusive of the springs is wild beyond many other wilderness areas. From a

Conundrum Hot Springs

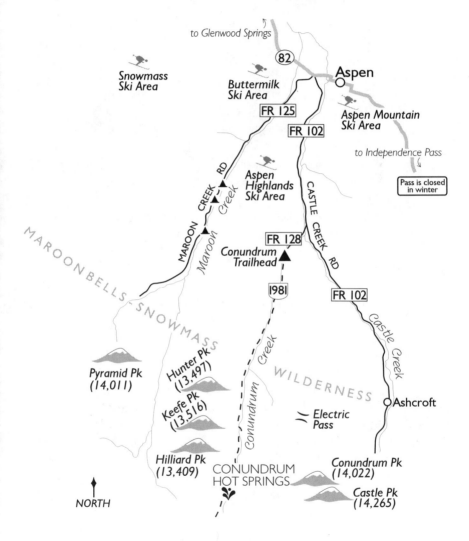

to Glenwood Springs

82

Aspen

Snowmass
Ski Area

Buttermilk
Ski Area

FR 125

Aspen Mountain
Ski Area

FR 102

to Independence Pass

Pass is closed
in winter

MAROON CREEK RD

Maroon Creek

Aspen
Highlands
Ski Area

CASTLE CREEK RD

FR 128

Conundrum
Trailhead

1981

FR 102

Castle Creek

MAROON BELLS-SNOWMASS

Conundrum Creek

WILDERNESS

Ashcroft

Electric
Pass

Pyramid Pk
(14,011)

Hunter Pk
(13,497)

Keefe Pk
(13,516)

Hilliard Pk
(13,409)

CONUNDRUM
HOT SPRINGS

Conundrum Pk
(14,022)

Castle Pk
(14,265)

NORTH

distance there is no sign of humans in the river basin. The weather can change from brilliant sun to snowflakes in a few minutes. Conundrum lives where nature reigns.

There are three soaking pools connected by a small hand-built rock waterway and long dark plastic pipe. The largest pool is about 15 feet across and about 4-1/2 feet deep—large enough for more than a dozen smiling soakers. The pool's edge is about a foot above the ground. Every seat around the rim has an astounding alpine view of sheer cliffs, snowy summits, and meadows. Conundrum Creek dribbles on down below, while above are Castle, Cathedral, Malamute, and Hayden Peaks. In back is the formidable ridge where Cooper, East Maroon, and Triangle Passes lead to Crested Butte. To the left are Hunter, Pyramid, and Precarious Peaks. The views are unparalleled in grandeur and scope.

The water temperature is a little cooler in the two lower pools, but still delightful. The springs' temperature is above 122 degrees, and the two lower pools are in the 100-plus-degree range, depending on the season.

The creek was named by puzzled prospectors in the late 1800s who found placer gold in the water and followed the stream upward in search of the mother lode. One of the prospectors commented, "It sure is a conundrum."

There's magic in all hot springs. Conundrum is so remote and in such untamed country that the enchantment is soul-binding. There's the lure of cross-country skiing up to the springs in the winter and camping. The warm water is a refuge, and the springs are a hidden friend shrouded in a great snowy blanket and in the particular silence of winter. There are those who spend the night in the spring's water and swear a good night's sleep is possible.

There's the lure of a clear night when the stars of stars are visible, when the Milky Way clouds the black sky like hot breath in the cold night. There's the enchantment of spring when the tundra around the hot springs greens weeks ahead of the dusty brown all around.

And there's the particular charm of the fall of 1995. The hillsides were ablaze with wildflowers. The grass and willows were still thick with green. Snow dusted the mountaintops. Speeding clouds dashed across the sky. The magic wavered when I counted the dozens of side trails tromped through the willows. The wind shifted and there was a burning whiff of urine and other human waste.

Perhaps that's the real conundrum of Conundrum Hot Springs—what spell, what charm will protect the place? Will the memories bind us all as its guardians?

The rules of wilderness are clear: no camping, horses, dogs, or human waste within 100 feet of pools, streams, and lakes. There were hoofprints, pawprints, and outhouse odors within 10 feet of the pools. No camping is allowed within a mile of the springs, but from the dents in the willow grove, the pounded ground, fire rings, and trees denuded of lower branches, it's obvious the rule is not heeded.

Smokey Bear and his minions will protect us from ourselves—there's precedent in other states for installing a permit system to limit the number of visitors to a hot springs or wilderness area. And should the pollution from human waste spread to the creek and river, the springs could be closed to everyone.

Go. Enjoy. Frolic and revel. Hardy souls swear by skiing up in the winter. But respect Conundrum Hot Springs for the marvel it is. And speak up for the springs when others treat it with contempt. By making the journey and floating in the springs' embrace, you do become its guardian.

Cottonwood Hot Springs

18999 Highway 306
Buena Vista 81211
(719) 395-6434
Open to the public; clothing optional; lodging; major credit cards
Where: From Buena Vista, take U.S. 24 north. At County Road
306, turn west (left) toward Cottonwood Pass. Drive about 5-1/2
miles. The hot springs sign will be on the right side of the road,
just before the gate used to close the road over Cottonwood Pass
in the winter.

A work in progress. By fall 1999, Cottonwood Hot Springs had
five stone-lined pools where the temperature ranged from 98
degrees to 108. And more were planned. There was Watsu, water,
Thai, and Japanese massage, and tepee lodging in the summer.
There were workshops in the Buffalo Dance and the Eclipse. It's
come a long way.

"The first time I saw the place, all the water was going into a
horse trough," says owner Cathy Manning who bought the then
Jump Steady Resort in 1986. The property was run down, had a
few hot tubs, but no springs pools. "I thought, 'I can fix this.'"

The fix is still in progress, and Cathy tells sobering tales that
would dissuade the faint-hearted and the under-financed from
buying a fixer-upper hot springs.

When she bought the resort, the buildings were dilapidated
and the hot tubs periodically violated state health standards for
cleanliness. She's fixed the tubs, spiffed up the front of the hotel,
worked on a series of hot springs pools, and found a way to raise
catfish in the pool outflows. But one woman, a series of volunteers,
and a few craftsmen who trade rooms for labor can't do everything.

Cottonwood has the look of an upgraded old western farm-
stead. The interior decor is classic 1950s. Cathy's wit appears in the

Buena Vista Area

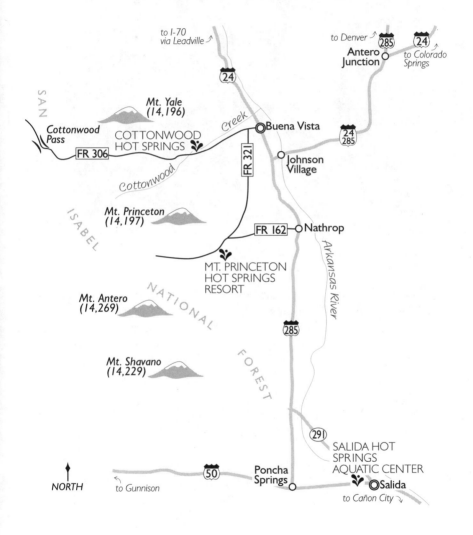

to I-70
via Leadville

to Denver

Antero
Junction

to Colorado
Springs

24

285

24

Mt. Yale
(14,196)

Creek

Buena Vista

24
285

Cottonwood
Pass

SAN

COTTONWOOD
HOT SPRINGS

FR 306

Cottonwood

FR 321

Johnson
Village

ISABEL

Mt. Princeton
(14,197)

FR 162

Nathrop

Arkansas River

NATIONAL

Mt. Antero
(14,269)

285

FOREST

Mt. Shavano
(14,229)

291

SALIDA HOT
SPRINGS
AQUATIC CENTER

NORTH

to Gunnison

50

Poncha
Springs

Salida

to Cañon City

Room for all ages at Cottonwood.

previously-loved teddy bear on every bed. There are no televisions or telephones in the rooms. She closed the restaurant because cooking took too much of her time. She wants to build a greenhouse to raise medicinal herbs. There's a herd of rabbits that wanders the grounds. And clothing is optional after dark between May 15 and September 15. The pools are open all night to guests at the hotel.

If it were the Old West, Cathy would own and run the local saloon. In fact, she did own and run a bar in Denver and has that bartender conviviality. She can speak in New Age maxims, the hippie cosmic karma idioms, solid working-class terms, and marketing whiz bang—all with the voice of absolute look-you-in-the-eye truth. She comes and goes at the springs, but leaves the day-to-day management to the staff. And she's studying hypnotherapy and past life regression.

The motel is at one end of the long lot and the pools, hot tubs, and fish ponds are at the other end. Between the pools and the private hot tub enclosures is a changing shelter. On the office wall, the Rules of Life are posted: "Love is all there is. Do Harm to No One. We are all one. . . ." There's also a reminder taped up: "Jesus is coming. Look busy."

The completed pools are lovely. The largest, built with smooth river rocks, is about 20 feet by 50 feet and 5 feet deep. Nirvana arrives at sunset, watching the light fade and turn the pool's ripples into a mosaic of pink, blue, and lavender.

The other four pools are smaller, about 20 feet in diameter with the same high quality rock work and balmy temperatures. A Japanese garden has taken over one corner of the yard, and flower gardens are planned. "The pools were designed to look like Buddha from the air," Cathy says.

Each of the three secluded hot tubs for private soakings has a good-sized deck, a redwood privacy fence, and a secluded river view—it's perfectly designed for lolling. A warm soak here, a cool plunge here, and then a nice half hour of hydrotherapy in the tub, and then, maybe, a massage.

"You see people come in here, and they're frazzled," Cathy says.

"It takes about four days to really lose that look. But after a couple days they're rejuvenated.

"Just watching the stars move across the sky is good for people," she says.

The rabbit herd is the latest installment of animal wildlife. Five years ago, it was chickens. The fowl roamed the parking lot, but not the pool area, during the day and produced eggs that Manning traded for fresh vegetables. She says she started with ducks, but they were rude to customers.

Soon after Colorado achieved statehood, the springs opened as a therapeutic resort run by a woman homeopathic healer. The buildings burned to the ground in 1885. The resort was rebuilt as a spa in 1911. In 1917 another fire razed that resort. The current two-story motel and restaurant were built by a previous owner in 1966, but were badly run down when Cathy came on the scene.

"Legend has it that there's a Ute curse on all owners, so white people can't be commercially successful here," Cathy says. She

Another wistful day at Cottonwood.

bought the resort with twelve rooms, three cabins, and a restaurant knowing it hadn't been successful.

"The world is a mess. I can't fix it," she says. "This I can fix."

Mount Princeton Hot Springs Resort

15870 County Road 162
Nathrop 81236
(719) 395-2361
www.mt.princeton.com
Open to the public; lodging; credit cards accepted
Where: On U.S. 285 between Buena Vista and Salida, turn west at the town of Nathrop onto County Road 162. Nathrop is about 6 miles south of Buena Vista. On County Road 162, drive 5 miles to the resort complex, which is on the left. See map, page 57.

Climbers who bag one of the nearby 14,000-feet tall Collegiate Peaks seek Mount Princeton's hot springs to salve the body. Rafters and kayakers who bounce down the icy Arkansas frolic in the hot springs along the banks of Chalk Creek and find steamy salvation. Explorers of the area's ghost towns, cross-country ski trails, and bike trails delight in the hot springs' civilized solace. And it's the only hot springs that rents out bathing suits.

The hot springs' pools are plain and clean. The 1850 bathhouse is functional and true to its Colorado Historic Register charter. The springs also heat the hotel.

There are nearly a dozen "hot spots"—person-sized pockets in the sand that are heated by small springs among the rocks in Chalk Creek. There is always a search for spaces among the bumpy rocks. The soaking pool, kept at about 102 degrees, is reached through a vintage entrance from the clapboard bathhouse and a plastic awning. The swimming pool, kept at about 92 degrees, is nestled between the canyon's steep walls and the wide creek.

The corps of lap swimmers hear Chalk Creek rumble as they ply the balmy waters. Each morning, local lap swimmers are always the first in the pool, a ritual they say keeps them limber into

The swimming pool isn't far from Chalk Creek at Mount Princeton Hot Springs Resort.

their eighties and nineties. Each has a way of keeping count of up to one hundred laps. One man uses an abacus; another woman leaves a water mark on the cement rim for each back-and-forth trip.

The Utes still had title to the land through a treaty when government surveyor D. H. Heywood laid claim to the springs in the mid-1800s. The Heywood Hot Springs House served area gold miners with a stagecoach stop, hotel, and the hot baths. The same stone-and-timber bathhouse that was built in 1850 is used today.

By 1880 there were fifty mines around the town of St. Elmo, up Chalk Creek from Mount Princeton. There was a Denver, South Park and Pacific Railroad stop at the springs, which was by then dubbed Mount Princeton Hot Springs. At its zenith in 1914, St. Elmo had a population of between five hundred to two thousand people. The top-producing mine, the Mary Murphy, had a crew of 250.

Founded in 1880 at 10,019 feet, St. Elmo grew steadily after the railroad reached the area and gold strikes continued. A fire in 1890 destroyed the town. The stream of gold from the mines carried the mining business, but the town never completely grew back. The railroad pulled out in 1926, and the Mary Murphy shut down after yielding about $14 million in gold. And the town fizzled to its current tiny population.

Down the road at the resort, the owner's fortunes rose and fell with St. Elmo's. By 1914, the newly named Antero Hotel at Mount Princeton was four stories high and boasted two hundred-foot towers, a golf course, and tennis courts. There were balconies, well-kept gardens, and a ballroom. The current forty-seven-room hotel was built on the foundation of the old hotel, which teetered on the edge of ruin from the neglect that started in the Depression.

In the 1950s, a group of Texans bought the hotel and moved it to Texas. At the same time, St. Elmo was vanishing to scavengers with pickup trucks and a fondness for weathered barn wood. The ghost town is worth visiting—there are still a few buildings and a sense of the isolation and primitive living conditions the miners endured.

Even farther down the road from Buena Vista, Mount Yale, Mount Princeton, Mount Harvard, and Mount Columbia form the Collegiate group of 14,000-foot peaks near Buena Vista. The Collegiates were so named by J. D. Whitney, who measured the massifs in 1869. Whitney graduated from Yale; most of the mapping party had attended Harvard, and one cartographer, Henry Gannett, had studied at Princeton.

Colorado has fifty-five Fourteeners, as the towering peaks are called. The Arkansas River Valley has six, including Mount Antero and Mount Shavano. Harvard and Columbia are the powerful peaks about 11 miles northwest of Buena Vista. Yale is 9 miles west of Buena Vista, and Princeton is 9 miles to the southwest. Climbers from every nation have come to the area for generations. In 1995 a pair of mountain endurance runners claimed the record for summiting each of the Fourteeners in about fifteen days.

Above the Mount Princeton resort, the Chalk Cliffs rise. Chalk Creek is named for the white powdery "flour" from the white limestone cliffs. With a properly positioned full moon, the cliffs glow and illuminate the canyon like a giant movie screen. Your imagination provides the picture show.

Salida Hot Springs Aquatic Center

410 West Rainbow Boulevard
Salida 81201
(719) 539-6738
Open to the public; credit cards not accepted
Where: The Salida Hot Springs Pool is located on U.S. 50 on the town's west side. U.S. 50 runs west and east through Salida's motel, restaurant, and commercial route. See map, page 57.

In Salida, all hot springs flow to the Salida Hot Springs Pool, even the springs from the neighboring town of Poncha Springs.

"Hooked on Hot Water" is the pool's unofficial motto. It's been Salida's motto too, since 1937, when a federal public works project, which employed two hundred, built the city pool and claimed Poncha's springs.

The pool is a standard city pool, with lap lanes, a kiddie adjunct, diving boards, and supportive banners for the local swim team. The temperature runs from 90 to 93 degrees. The large soaking pool holds water at about 100 degrees, and the kiddie pool stays at about 96 degrees.

And there are six private old-style soaking tubs. Each of the tubs is about the size of a closet. Cement stairs lead down into the small vault that becomes a tub when filled with water. Pull the lever and out blasts 113-degree water with a forceful flow rarely seen in modern bathtubs. The tubs are large enough for stretching out or for sitting on the stairs. Or one can stand in water up to the chin. There's nothing better after climbing one of the area's 14,000-foot peaks, or rafting the chilly waters of the Arkansas.

The tubs pleasantly call to mind the 1940s, with tiny wood-framed windows above. The fresh white paint is hygienically reassuring, but there are no flashy water jets. Down the hall there's the sound

A view of Poncha Springs long before the Salida Hot Springs Pool began borrowing water. (Photograph courtesy Colorado Historical Society)

of sloshing and laughter. Reposing in the water, decades vanish. Is it Humphrey Bogart's voice or Bette Davis's laugh?

The actual hot springs that feed the pool are located 5 miles west of town, in Poncha Springs, where about forty-five springs gurgle up. The main springs are housed in a blockhouse and securely fenced. A few springs surface along the river on private property and also are fenced against trespassing.

Spanish explorers passed through the area looking for gold and Indian slaves. Later came the trappers, and then, in 1807, Lieutenant Zebulon Pike stopped by during his exploration of the West and spent the Christmas of 1806 in the area.

The Utes used the springs at Poncha for centuries. In 1863, miners and homesteaders starting building cabins near the springs, ignoring the Utes' protests and various treaties. Early Indian agents pacified the Utes with flour, sugar, old army uniforms, and bib overalls.

Mount Ouray, Mount Shavano, and Mount Antero near Poncha and Salida were named for Ute leaders. In 1881, the Utes were moved to reservations in southwestern Colorado, near Durango and Cortez, and in Utah.

As more settlers arrived, they erected tent cities around the springs for those seeking "the cure." Miners and railroad workers joined the crowd at the Poncha bathing pool in the late 1860s, and Henry Weber is credited with digging the first official pool in 1868.

Up north in the Arkansas River Valley, Leadville emerged as the Silver King. In 1878, $2 million in ore was wrested from the high mountains on the shoulder of the Continental Divide. The potential for profits was mouthwatering, but the nearest railhead was 75 miles away. Prices for food were princely, and a barrel of whiskey reportedly ran $1,500. Both the Denver and Rio Grande and the Santa Fe started work on separate rail lines in 1878. Their conflict moved to court, where lawyers warred over who had the right to build the track. In 1880, a court in Boston gave the Denver and Rio Grande permission to start work. By year's end, the track stretched from the new town of Salida up the Arkansas Valley and into Leadville. The population near Leadville jumped from five hundred in 1878 to twenty-four thousand in 1880—second only to Denver at the time.

A. C. Hunt, a former Colorado territorial governor, worked for the Denver and Rio Grande. Although Poncha was an established town, he decided that what became Salida was a better spot for the railroad town. He and his wife named the community Salida, which is Spanish for gateway or exit.

Salida also became a supply center for the mining camps, including those near Crested Butte and Gunnison. Life was a bit rough at first, with lynchings, shootings, and general lawlessness. During a single two-week period that ended on July 8, 1890, nineteen prisoners escaped from the jail.

The town grew so fast that residents proposed making Salida the state capital. Salida abandoned the plan when Buena Vista won the county-seat designation by one thousand votes. But Salida prospered as a mining-supply town and agricultural community.

Five miles west, in Poncha, the posh two-hundred-room Jackson Hotel had opened in 1878 to serve the spa's visitors. The hotel belonged to Henry Jackson, who had left his native Kentucky in search of the "garden of Eden." He'd picked Poncha Springs because the hot springs already were drawing people from all over the world. Recorded in the hotel guest book are the signatures of Billy the Kid in 1881, Susan B. Anthony in 1882, Frank and Jesse James in 1882, President Ulysses Grant and Rudyard Kipling in 1884, and Alexander Graham Bell in 1886. However, there is some suspicion that locals signed the names in jest, although Kipling did marry a girl from Salida, Grant and Bell visited Colorado, and Anthony gave a speech on women's suffrage in the area.

The hotel is still in operation, but the springs were routed in 1938 to Salida, which paid $160,000 to install a water line and build the pool. Salida had watched Poncha prosper and slide through mining busts on the magic carpet of spas and hotels around the springs. Salida planned to lease the water, but jumped at the chance to buy the rights when two Poncha men put the springs up for sale for only $40,000.

Today the Salida Hot Springs Pool is the state's largest indoor hot springs pool. "The old time residents of Salida always maintained that the bringing of the water to Salida would make the city's future secure," predicted the *Salida Daily Mail* on June 23, 1938. That was the day the town pool filled with water from Poncha.

Cement Creek Ranch

Crested Butte 81224
(970) 349-6512
www.awdcva.com/ccr
Registered guests only; credit cards not accepted
Where: From Gunnison, take Colorado 135 north toward Crested
Butte for 21 miles. At Cement Creek Road turn east, and travel on
the dirt road for 5 miles, past the Cement Creek Campground.
Cement Creek Ranch is on the right side of the road and has a sign
at the entrance.

The water is a tepid 75 degrees, but the spectacular setting is
all yours.

Cement Creek Ranch, set in a nearly pristine valley surrounded
by the Gunnison National Forest, has only one guest cabin. The
owner lives out of shouting range, and the ranch hand lives on the
other side of the swimming pool. The view from the guest cabin's
porch is mountain meadow, 13,379-foot Italian Mountain, waterfalls, and a crystal clear creek with no condos, power lines, or roads
in sight.

While the hot pool—or rather, warm pool—is more of an
amenity than a main attraction, it's in splendid isolated environs
that offer hiking, mountain biking, rock climbing, cross-country
skiing, and fishing. The stream and surrounding 121 acres are pri-
vately owned, which guarantees privacy and quiet in the valley.

"It's not really a hot springs, although it's a nice attribute,"
owner Dave Baxter says. "The calling card is that up here, you're
by yourself."

The remote valley at 9,200 feet wasn't homesteaded until
1923. In 1963, the owner built eight cabins, but only one has been
renovated for year-round rental. The ranch manager lives in another cabin, but the others are empty. Baxter, who bought the place

Gunnison Area

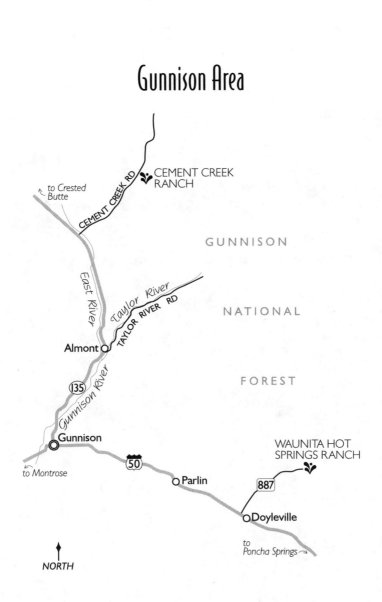

to Crested Butte

CEMENT CREEK RD

CEMENT CREEK RANCH

GUNNISON

East River

Taylor River

TAYLOR RIVER RD

NATIONAL

Almont

135

Gunnison River

FOREST

Gunnison

WAUNITA HOT SPRINGS RANCH

to Montrose

50

Parlin

887

Doyleville

to Poncha Springs

NORTH

A hot springs marsh at Cement Creek Ranch.

in 1991, isn't interested in running a dude ranch, although there are corrals for guests who bring horses.

"People get up here and they think they're pioneers," says Dave.

The pool isn't chlorinated and it sits next to a marshy meadow created by other hot springs. The corrals and guest cabin add an Old West ambiance to the pool-deck's view—like John Wayne's summer ranch.

The cabin has a gas fireplace for heat, full kitchen, a bath with a shower and a tub, and sleeps six with a sleeper couch in the living room.

Should the rustic, rugged privacy prove oppressive, the bright lights and restaurants of Crested Butte are about 12 miles, or twenty minutes, away.

Waunita Hot Springs Ranch

8007 County Road 887
Gunnison 81230
(970) 641-1266
www.waunita.com

Registered guests only May to November with a six-day minimum stay; open to the public mid-December to April; credit cards not accepted

Where: From Gunnison, drive 19 miles east on U.S. 50. At the sign for Waunita Hot Springs, turn left (north) on County Road 887. Drive 8 miles to the ranch, which is on the left side of the road. See map, page 69.

The Pringles believe that Waunita Hot Springs is a serendipity. Rod and Junelle Pringle bought the guest ranch in 1962 and emphasize the western experience of horseback riding, hayrides, square dancing, cookouts, fishing, and the splendid scenery offered by the Gunnison National Forest. The ranch focuses on family vacations. No alcohol is permitted, but the cookie jar is always full.

"The hot springs and the pool are amenities, not attractions," says Junelle. "It's a serendipity."

The springs are about 175 degrees, among the hottest in the state. The pool is kept at 95 degrees.

Local folklore, based on Ute stories, says Waunita was a Ute maiden who loved a Shoshone warrior who was killed in battle. The maiden died of grief, and when she was buried in a small cave the springs emerged from her tears. In the hills around the ranch, three generations of Pringles have found tepee rings and arrowheads.

John C. Frémont's survey party came through the area in 1843, and miners were pouring in by the 1860s—and bathing in the hot springs. The railroad arrived in 1879 to take ore out and carry

Waunita Springs, poised on the brink of greatness, around 1900. (Photograph courtesy Colorado Historical Society)

settlers in. There was a well-worn trail to the site by 1880, and the Utes were evicted in 1881.

In 1882, Charles Elgin built a log hotel next to the lower springs and bestowed his own name on the springs. By 1885 there was a two-story hotel, a bathhouse, and a swimming pool. A stagecoach ferried train passengers from Doyleville to the hot springs for $1.50. The trip from Gunnison via train and stagecoach took about three hours. Today it's about a half-hour car trip.

By 1884, Dr. Charles Davis of Chicago had bought most of the upper and lower springs property next to Elgin's, renamed the area Waunita, and waited for serendipity to strike. For twelve years locals enjoyed the springs for picnics, dances, and rodeos. Invalids were the only out-of-town guests. In the 1890s, Davis began transforming the springs into an international spa with orchestra musicians, spirituality, and a fevered temperance.

"What is the matter with European Civilization?" Davis wrote in 1923. "Through centuries of alcohol saturation, the human brain has been made incapable of evolving those thoughts which make for progress. The medical profession will solve the problem by condemning alcohol," he went on. "What will they substitute in place of alcohol? Radium water."

He believed the springs water contained radium, the radioactive element whose use was pioneered by Marie Curie. Later tests didn't find radium, but they did confirm that Waunita's water temperature was among the hottest in the state.

During the early 1900s and the height of America's belief that Curie had found a cure for all ills, Davis brought patients and friends to Waunita Hot Springs by train, built a forty-room hotel, bottled the radium water for sale, built a sanitarium, and ran a stage line to the train in Doyleville. He also wrote about treating patients with radium water for cancer, excessive menstrual bleeding, tuberculosis, malaria, ulcers, syphilis, and tonsillitis. Guests drank the water every two hours.

"What is it?" he wrote in the *American Journal of Clinical Medicine* in 1921. "It may yet be demonstrated scientifically that radium is the connecting link between what the scientist calls matter and what the theologian calls spirit."

Davis died in 1928. The Depression and World War II cut off resort business. By the late 1940s, vacations by car had replaced the traditional two weeks at a resort. In 1948 Davis's daughter and her husband renovated the buildings but sold out to local investors in 1952. Waunita remained vacant and unused for five years, until 1957, when Carl Bolin bought Waunita and turned the resort into a youth sports camp. Rod and Junelle Pringle bought the ranch in 1962.

The Pringles, their son Ryan and daughter-in-law Tammy all work at the ranch, which is family-oriented with modern resort amenities, home-style cooking, a Christian atmosphere, family-style meals, and an alpine setting untouched by commercialism. For city kids, it's a chance to throw rocks in the creek, chase frogs, fish, get to know a horse, run up a hill, meet real cowboys, and look for arrowheads. "Waunita is a natural playground—and there are no poisonous snakes!" says the brochure.

Adults enjoy the riding, the scenery, the four-wheel-drive trips, fishing, rafting, and the family emphasis in all activities. That includes soaking in the 95-degree pool at the end of a day's ride on the range.

As you drive out, just before you reach the highway a tall iron sign with a cowboy figure reads "Happy Trails." A little serendipity for the road.

Desert Reef Beach Club

1194 County Road 110
P.O. Box 503
Florence 81240
(719) 784-6134

Members only; clothing optional; open Wednesdays, Thursdays, Saturdays, and Sundays; credit cards accepted

Where: Located 2 miles east of Florence. From U.S. 50 between Pueblo and Cañon City just west of Penrose, take Colorado 115 south toward Florence. After 2.5 miles, turn left onto Colorado 120 and drive for about a mile. At the tall wooden cactus sign reading "Desert Reef Beach Club," turn right onto County Road 110. Drive for about a mile through the piñon and juniper rangeland and follow the "DRBC" signs.

Just when you're convinced there is no there there, there's the Desert Reef Beach Club. It's a desert rose of sorts that makes the journey through three ecosystems and down remote gravel roads worth the time. Set in the desert, the club taps into an artesian well, which was left by oil drilling to create a lovely spa with a propensity for humor.

There's the story about the bobcat that came to visit. The large feline, apparently dumped in the remote area by someone who changed his mind about having a wild animal as a pet, wandered onto the pool deck, checked out the bathers, purred when petted, and waited patiently for the Colorado Division of Wildlife to arrive. Nude and besuited bathers alike offered sandwiches and water to the skinny animal.

When the DOW officer arrived, he hadn't realized the Desert Reef was a clothing-optional pool. He nearly walked into a fishpond. Everyone laughed.

Quiet and solitude envelop bathers at the Desert Reef Beach Club.

Cañon City Area

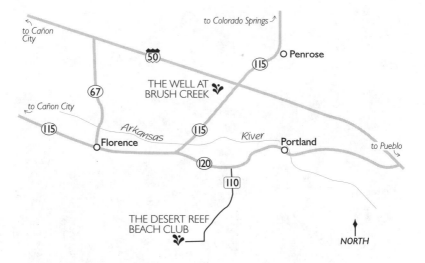

The cat was captured, rehabilitated, and released to the wild.

Bob Kellner and L. J. Conrad bought the land, the calcium-lined ditch created by the artesian well's flows, and the 133-degree water source in 1985. They've created a pool, waterfall, greenhouse, office, fishponds, volleyball field, and oasis with a mountain backdrop.

There's also the story about the ambulance. A member was having trouble breathing and an ambulance was called. The dispatcher knew the Desert Reef was clothing-optional. "Within fifteen minutes, we had two ambulances and nine paramedics," says L. J. "The members were smart. They'd put their clothes on. Those paramedics were pretty disappointed. We got a good laugh."

The 36- by 50-foot pool was designed and built by L. J., along with the waterfall in the corner. The fall's stone work is composed of the honeycombed calcium deposits left by the well's flows in the ditch. The chunks of rock are the size and weight of Volkswagens but have delicate pockets of calcium nodes, clusters of white calcium flowers, and tiny caverns.

The pool's water is cooled to the 90s during the summer for comfort. L. J. routed the flows through a gridwork of pipes under a sand floor to create the greenhouse. The building is used summer and winter for parties and is rented out to community groups on the three days a week the pool is closed. "The community laughs and giggles at the nudies, but they'll come out and use it for parties," says Bob.

An artesian well taps groundwater that is naturally under pressure and flows to the surface without pumping. The word *artesian* comes from Artois, a province in France where artesian wells were first drilled in the 1100s.

The calcium deposits, which can cut skin like razor blades, and the water temperature deterred locals from using the hot water after the initial drilling in the 1940s. The wells were exploratory oil wells, and oil pumpers still dot the area around Desert Reef.

Since Bob and L. J. have improved the place, local kids try to sneak in at night. There's a visual joke about that. Metal sculpture and ceramics from local artists decorate the grounds. In the earth berm that surrounds the club to ensure privacy, dozens of life-sized ceramic heads are partially buried. "Those are the people that have tried to sneak in. We calcified them in the water and buried them," says Bob. "Every time it rains, the dirt washes off a few."

Although Desert Reef is members only, there's a little space available on some days for nonmembers who call ahead. However, "If you don't call, don't come," said both Bob and L. J. Like most clothing-optional hot springs, the Desert Reef doesn't advertise much. Word of mouth and guidebooks keep the membership at about two hundred, with visitors from all over the world.

"Happiness is no tan line," reads a bumper sticker in the office. For nonmembers, there must be a female for every male to prevent groups of guys dropping in to gape. The male-female ratio doesn't mean couples only. "The only basis for discrimination here is if you are a jerk, then you're gone," said L. J., who remembers people he threw out ten years ago and still bars them from the pool. L. J. and

Bob aren't nudists or naturists, just businessmen who realized they had more customers on days that were clothing-optional.

Once you're there, you may wonder what else is there in the middle of nowhere. Cutting across the high-mountain desert is the Royal Gorge, a miles-long slit in the earth with the Arkansas River glinting at the bottom. The suspension bridge over the great gash is good for a few gasps, but the incline rail trip down into the gorge is the ultimate scary ride.

When silver was discovered in the Upper Arkansas in 1877, the Santa Fe and the Denver and Rio Grande started to build competing rail lines, although there was only enough business for one. There were acts of sabotage and court suits. The Santa Fe called in former frontier marshal Bat Masterson. Former governor A. C. Hunt rallied two hundred men for a posse. The railroad war raged for ten days, and the Rio Grande won.

Today the Arkansas, which cut the canyon, is the busiest rafting waterway in the country, with thousands riding the white water through spectacular scenery, including Brown's Canyon.

At the Desert Reef the waters are calm and there are no shrieks of terror. But Bob and L. J. tell a story about when L. J.'s father came to visit. L. J. had reminded his father three times on the drive to the Desert Reef that it was clothing-optional.

"He got changed and went out to the pool and came whizzing back into the office. 'People don't have any clothing on!'" says L. J. His father went back out and, after a few hours, had a good time after all.

The Well at Brush Creek

0001 Malibu Boulevard
Highway 50 at Penrose
Penrose 81240
(719) 372-9250
Membership club, visitors welcome; clothing optional; tent camp-
sites; credit cards accepted
Where: From the crossroads of Colorado 115 (between Colorado
Springs and Florence) and U.S. 50 (between Pueblo and Canon
City), take U.S. 50 west for 1 mile. Look for the American flag fly-
ing on the left (south). Turn left at the flag and follow the short
road to The Well, which is visible from U.S. 50. See map, page 78.

This place is one of a kind. Consider bubble night. Every
Monday night, members and guests bring bottles of bubble
bath and fill the 70-foot-diameter pool with bubbles. The pool is
closed Tuesday for cleaning, so there's a method to the bubble
madness—the bubbles overflow the pool and perform the first
rinse. The forty or fifty bubble devotees cavort in 3- and 4-feet-
deep waves of foam. And since The Well is clothing-optional, bubble dancing enjoys a renaissance.

In the summer of 1995 The Well was retro-funky-hip in a
friendly 1960s kind of way.

The Well is enjoying a rebirth after its former owner ran out of
money in 1985 and the Resolution Trust Corporation took over.
During its eight years of federal trust ownership, The Well was
closed. The once well-groomed resort fell into disrepair. Today, two
years after it reopened in 1993, The Well is still down at the heels.
Child-high weeds replace the long dead lawns, fine mesh webbing
over rough boards creates some shade in the treeless rangeland,
and the office is reminiscent of gas stations of the 1950s.

Behind the cash register, manager Grover Simpson loads hundreds of handgun shells. He and a friend shoot through the ammunition once a month at a shooting range, and he reloads in between customers. The prominently displayed hobby doesn't encourage riffraff, the bane of clothing-optional springs.

The pool and showers and changing areas are clean. The cabana used for massages is nicely renovated. All health department inspections are current. The people are nice and gently advocate the virtues of going bare. There's no pressure to go nude, but there's a little bemusement over bathing-suited patrons. The regulars offer some witty observations about how social paradigms shift when people don't wear clothing.

"You strip clothes off and you don't know if you're talking to a doctor or a judge or a policeman or a general," says Grover.

"The classes break down," says Randy Jenkins, who has worked at The Well through the last few changes in proprietorship.

The Well is literally right off Highway 50 between Pueblo and Canon City. An American flag and a sign marks the turn. The fenced enclave is the only structure for miles in the rolling rangeland. The Well has three simple rules: no glass, no drugs, and no creeps.

"We throw out the drunks. We throw out the rowdies. We throw out people sharking the girls," Grover says. He says The Well is clothing-optional because there are plenty of public pools for kids but few pools that offer year-round nude tanning and swimming.

Annual memberships in 1999 were $150 for a local single, $195 for a local couple, $100 for a long-distance single, and $125 for a long-distance couple. "Local" includes Pueblo, Colorado Springs, Canon City, and Trinidad. Members pay $5 per visit, and their guests pay $8 each. For a nonmember, one-time-only walk-in, the price is $10. There are camping spaces, but no RV hookups or other lodging available.

The Canon City area is also home to several federal and state prison complexes that don't attract many casual visitors. The multi-building corrections complexes dot the high-mountain desert in the area, glowing through the night. Very few prisoners have successfully breached the walls, barbed wire fences, and security guards.

There is one offbeat roadside attraction that doesn't turn up in many guidebooks—the Colorado Territorial Prison Museum in Canon City. The exhibits are located in recreations of inmate cells, and the displays show the evolution of the penal system. There's even a gas chamber and a gift shop full of inmate-made items. The best-seller is a "State Prison" mug painted with inmate stripes.

It's rough country for a hot spring. But The Well isn't a hot spring. Conoco Oil created the artesian well in 1924 while drilling for oil. The water began flowing at 2,000 feet and the oil company took their rigs elsewhere. A livestock tank claimed the flows for cattle.

In 1956, Hazel Higgins bought the land and the spring and built the pool and a home as a getaway for herself and her husband, Charlie Higgins, a successful Colorado Springs stockbroker. Charlie Higgins died in the 1970s and Hazel rented out the complex until the 1980s, when she sold it. The new owner lost it to the Resolution Trust Corporation in 1985, and The Well remained closed until the current owner reopened it in 1993.

The artesian spring water comes out of the ground at 108 degrees. The large pool stays in the high 90s depending on the season, and the soaking tub set in the middle of the pool is 108 degrees. The altitude is 5,200 feet, but The Well is located in a desert valley considered part of the state's Banana Belt and accommodates tanning zealots nearly year-round. The facility is closed Tuesdays for cleaning and Wednesdays for private parties.

"Warning: Beyond this point you may encounter nude sunbathers," reads the sign on the door to the pool. Simpson has a few good stories about people who didn't know it was a clothing-optional pool or who hadn't counted on so many bathers being nude. "Once you get used to seeing the naked body, there's nothing to it," says Grover. "I love the freedom. If I want to go swimming I can just drop my drawers and jump in."

Orvis Hot Springs

1585 County Road 3
Ridgway 81432
(970) 626-5324
Open to the public; lodging; clothing optional; credit cards accepted
Where: On U.S. 550 between Montrose and Ouray. The springs are located near Ridgway on the west side of U.S. 550. About one mile south of Ridgway, turn west at the "Orvis Hot Springs" sign onto County Road 3.

The yellow brick road through the West's hot springs leads to Orvis. The road's end goes through a door, past four private tub rooms, past the changing areas, and out a back door. Then the road swings left and, suddenly, the 5-foot-deep, 30-foot-wide pool reveals itself. And should the bather want a change, there's a cooling plunge next to the pool.

The wildflower beds, the San Juan Mountains that frame the scene, and the clarity of the water quickly convince the visitor that Orvis is *the* place. The pool is sunken, so it's invisible from the road and there's a cooling plunge next to the pool so bathers can flip back and forth. Baby lambs in the pasture across the fence impart a bucolic beauty. The view is capital "S" spectacular.

There were tractor parts in the pool in 1986 when Jeff and Andy Kerbel bought it. The couple's vision saw past the two shacks

Pastoral splendor at the Orvis Hot Springs.

next to the hot springs swamp to today's splendid sight. The Kerbels had an enormous amount of energy, which was poured into recontouring, re-landscaping, and reinventing the springs. For several years, he toured hot springs all over the U.S. a few months each year. He's a friendly, funny, living guidebook to the places, people, and stories that revolve about hot springs.

Orvis is a locals' springs, drawing most of its clientele from towns along the Uncompahgre River Valley that are connected by U.S. 550. The staff knows most visitors by name. In every conversation, Kim's insights and quips about stress, relaxation, life, hot springs, and the future turn the plain into champagne. The greater social landscape is rarefied. Poolside conversations move about the theater in Telluride, movie star sightings, changes in county zoning, debates about the best masseuse, emerging therapy techniques, and how other hot springs are faring.

Orvis also has a sauna with a small, outdoor soaking pool at 105 to 108 degrees. There's also a nice lodge with six rooms that share two baths and a camping area. Alcohol is barred from the premises.

Ouray Area

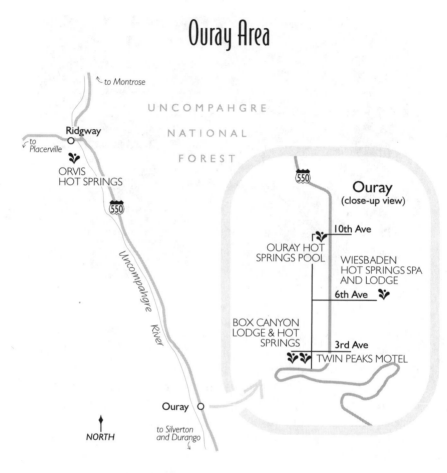

to Montrose

UNCOMPAHGRE

NATIONAL

FOREST

Ridgway

to Placerville

ORVIS
HOT SPRINGS

550

550

Ouray
(close-up view)

10th Ave

OURAY HOT
SPRINGS POOL

WIESBADEN
HOT SPRINGS SPA
AND LODGE

6th Ave

BOX CANYON
LODGE & HOT
SPRINGS

3rd Ave

TWIN PEAKS MOTEL

Uncompahgre River

Ouray

NORTH

to Silverton
and Durango

Ridgway is a Colorado bellwether. The small town is poised at the convergence of the road to Telluride, the road to Ouray, and the road to Grand Junction (via Montrose). Ridgway's own growing pains—the population nearly doubled in the early 1990s—are a microcosm of the state's rapid population expansion. Ralph Lauren owns a ranch nearby. Dennis Weaver has lived in Ridgway since 1988 and owns a dance hall. Another local ranch is a favored backdrop for Marlboro commercials, and the handsome cowboy smokers turn up in the town's cafes during filming.

In 1993 newcomers wanted a twenty-four-hour supermarket. Locals wanted their quiet night sky. The locals won—that time.

Orvis is a clothing optional spring. To avoid problems with gawkers, Orvis never advertises; there are no brochures nor business cards. It is a place where locals bring their children. There hasn't been a problem for years, but if anyone crosses the boundary between enjoying the scenery and leering, eviction is immediate and permanent. "Skinny Dipping isn't a spectator sport," reads a sign in the lobby. Guests are advised to wear a robe or a towel on the grounds except when in the pool area.

Clothing is required in the indoor soaking pool, which is ringed by plants and windows. It is three feet deep and about twenty-five feet across. The favored pastime there involves reading and soaking simultaneously in the 103–105 degree water.

The private tubs are newly lined with Mexican blue tile and are as big as extra-long double beds. Each tub has a high window providing views of the mountains. Temperatures range from 102 to 109 degrees. The tubs are scrubbed everyday. The outdoor pool is closed and cleaned on the first day of each new moon.

The hot springs have hosted many bathers and soakers over time. The water gushes out at 127 degrees, so the Utes dug shallow canals from the main pool to a circle of smaller pools that were then cool enough for bathing. *Aka-paa-garu-ri*, or "red water standing," was the Ute term for the springs, which were later renamed for Orvis, a settler.

From the 1860s on, settlers and miners moved to the area. The Uncompahgre Valley became the last holding ground for Chief

Ouray, the Ute leader. "For as long as the rivers might run and the grasses might grow," the Valley was to belong to the Ute, according to an early treaty that acknowledged Ute ownership of the springs and surrounding land. But even before Congress nullified the treaty, gold strikes near the town of Ouray led the U.S. Army to remove the Utes in 1881. Dozens of people had squatted, settled, and claimed the land. Tom Goshorn squatted on the land around the springs in the early 1870s and sold it to Sarah and Lewis Orvis who dubbed it the Hot Springs Ranch in 1877. "We paid him a team of young Hambleton mares, harness and wagon and one hundred dollars in cash," wrote Sarah Eloisa Randall Jarvis Orvis about the purchase of land from Goshorn.

Conflicts between squatters and the Utes were infrequent. Ouray chose instead to pursue the Utes' treaty rights with the U.S. Army and federal representatives, but all to no avail. He died the year before the Utes were exiled.

Lewis Orvis arrived in 1882 and completed work on the Orvis Plunge—a popular term at the time for a soaking pool—in 1919. He added a lake for fishing and a club house, where community dances, church gatherings, and school graduations were held through the 1940s. Over the years, a series of owners added hydrotherapy and chiropractic offices, but the dilapidated facilities were headed for foreclosure in 1986 when the Kerbels bought the property, and the rest is happy hot springs history.

Ouray Hot Springs Pool

1000 Main Street
P.O. Box 468
Ouray 81427-0468
(970) 325-4638
Open to the public; credit cards accepted
Where: From U.S. 50 through Ouray, the hot springs pool is on the town's north side, toward Montrose, at 10th Avenue. The pool and parking are on the west side of the road. See map, page 86.

In Ouray, life revolves around the pool. Gold and silver mining put this remote town at 7,800 feet on the map. The town was named for Chief Ouray, who counseled the Uncompahgre Utes against warfare when thousands of settlers came to stay. The hot springs and the city pool keep the tourist dollars flowing into the spectacular mountain valley.

The 250- by 150-foot oval pool contains about 1 million gallons of water and is divided into seven sections—an aqua relish plate with steaming liquid in each compartment. The water's temperatures range from 82 to 105 degrees to please everyone at the city-owned pool.

Even mundane laps become magical when the swimmer looks up at the Milky Way stretched between steep mountainsides. Bathers move between the sections in slow and constant procession, questing for the perfect temperature. Townsfolk swim or soak on lunch breaks and after work. Real estate deals, investments, and business sales are negotiated within the pool's confines.

Ouray's nickname is Little Switzerland. The American bather is as likely to hear English as German, French, or Swedish. In the summer, up to eight hundred people take a dip on the busiest days.

Ouray Hot Springs Pool is the life of Ouray.

In the winter, the numbers shrink in proportion to the town's one thousand residents.

Ouray is primarily a summer-vacation destination. Many of its businesses close during the winter months. Telluride is about an hour away, and overflow from the resort town has kept some Ouray lodges and restaurants open through the winter. The pool remains open all year. During the snowy months, on the night of each full moon the pool closes late so bathers can enjoy a municipally provided lunar experience. The full moon's light bounces off the snowy peaks that circle the town. The pool's water catches the moonbeams, and all is bathed in a pearly light.

"The pool is what makes this city survive," said Bob Freier, Ouray's parks and recreation director. The pool's proceeds pay for six other parks in town.

Gus Begole and Jack Eckles were looking for the glitter of gold and silver, not moonlight, when they ventured up the valley in July of 1875. In the scenic mountain basin they located the Cedar and Clipper lodes at the south end of the contemporary town. In September they went to Howardsville to get supplies, telling mining parties along the way about the finds. When they returned to Ouray in August, the pair found other miners working claims. They also discovered a claim to a patch of closely spaced parallel veins near the surface on 40 acres about a mile from town. Their farming backgrounds came to the fore, and they named the claim Mineral Farms.

Howardsville's fortunes waned as mining declined. All that remains is a few log cabins inhabited by a few hearty families. Ouray's fate was far better. By 1876 there were four hundred people in Ouray and more than two hundred dwellings. Its gold and silver ore was processed in Silverton, about 18 miles away, which meant the road was always crowded with burros and mules.

By treaty, the land belonged to the Utes. The southern tribes were "managed" from the Uncompahgre agency near Montrose. After the northern Ute bands rebelled when troops marched onto their land by killing eleven people in the Meeker Massacre in 1879, the U.S. retaliated with a treaty that forced the Utes to cede all of Colorado.

The Utes weren't willing to sign or leave. The treaty required three-fourths of the adult male Utes to consent to it before it could be ratified. Otto Mears, who had established mail routes into the area and later built toll roads, paid every adult male Ute $2 for his signature. Within a few months the treaty was ratified.

By 1881 the Utes were gone and Ouray's population was close to three thousand. The silver mines sustained Ouray until the 1893 silver crash. In the 1890s there were about thirty-five saloons and a red-light district on Second Street that featured The Temple of Music and The Bird Cage. Many of the proud Victorian hotels, homes, businesses, and city buildings constructed in the glory days are still standing.

The silver crash occurred when the precious metal was de-monetized by Congress. Since many of the Ouray mines also con-tained gold, the mining operations switched over to survive. In 1896, the legendary Camp Bird gold mine opened southwest of town and yielded about $5,000 a day. Tom Walsh, its founder and owner, sold Camp Bird in 1902 for $5.2 million.

The road is rough—four-wheel-drive only—but Camp Bird Mine and a dozen others are accessible from Ouray. There are tours and rental jeeps available in town. Gazing at the ruins of the Camp Bird Mine after reaching the site via a narrow road along a steep cliff, one marvels at the men and mules who worked the shafts.

While it was owned by Walsh, the Camp Bird Mine produced about $22 million in gold and financed the building of top-quality quarters for about four hundred men, who enjoyed steam heat, electric lights, and marble countertops in the lavatories.

The Camp Bird Mine also turned Walsh into a diplomat and world traveler. He purchased the Hope diamond for his wife. His daughter, Evelyn Walsh McLean, inherited the legendary gem. McLean, whose first child was known as "The Hundred-Million Dollar Baby," lived in Washington, D.C., and entertained American tycoons, crowned heads of Europe, and President Harding. She also wrote the book *Daddy Struck it Rich*.

As the town's fortunes prospered, so did the hot springs' im-mediate environs. Although the springs near Box Canyon had a bathhouse in the 1880s, the town's pool site was part of Francis Carney's brickyard. He excavated the mud around the spring to make bricks, and over time the springs filled the void. The town added goldfish and ballfields after the brickyard moved and declared the area a park in 1903. During World War I, the demand for food mandated that the ballfield be planted in potatoes. The name Radium Springs Park was bestowed in 1920, at the height of America's love affair with radioactivity.

In about 1924, a local man vacationing in Florida shipped an alligator to the town of Ouray as a prank. The gator resided first in the city hall basement and then in a fenced pond in the park, where he was joined by a second alligator. The city opened the big pool in 1929, the year floods tore out businesses, homes, and part of the pool. The gators, known as Al and Allie, survived the inundation, but soon after Al attacked Allie and inflicted fatal injuries. Shortly after Al escaped, was recaptured, and died a few months later. A sad fate indeed for 'gators residing in alpine towns.

The pool's main spring pours forth at 157 degrees. A secondary spring is 118 degrees, so cold water is added to prevent parboiled patrons. No chlorine is used.

On a winter's night, steam from the hot springs engulfs the north side of Ouray. Bathers appear and disappear in the mists. Submerged in the water, soakers can claim a far corner within the fog, hide from other visitors, and scan the constellations in solitude and warmth.

The Wiesbaden Hot Springs Spa and Lodge

625 5th Avenue
P.O. Box 349
Ouray 81427
(970) 325-4347
Open to the public; lodging; credit cards accepted
Where: In the town of Ouray, turn east off Main Street (U.S. 550) at 6th Avenue. Drive 3 blocks. The Wiesbaden is at the northeast corner of 6th Avenue and 5th Street. See map, page 86.

Surrounded by towering peaks, The Wiesbaden has the look of a European spa and the hospitality of a family lodge.

The Wiesbaden's heart and soul shimmer in a large cave beneath the spa building. Water pours from the spring at 120 degrees, filling a pool and emanating steam that fills the bedroom-sized chamber. In the quiet of the natural vapor cave, the pulse of the spring and a rhythmic inhaling and exhaling are the only sounds. The vapor, the heat, and the pool meld together and the bather merges with the springs.

No wonder the Wiesbaden's springs were part of the last parcel of land relinquished by the Colorado Utes. "Shining Mountains" was the Ute description of the San Juan Mountains, which surround Ouray at 7,760 feet.

Those same shining mountains loom above The Wiesbaden's outdoor pool. Owner Linda Wright-Minter has turned the spa into a place of healing for the body and the soul. Native Americans frequent The Wiesbaden for healing ceremonies. "The Wiesbaden cave has a history of spirituality which gives a strong presence now," says Linda. The Wiesbaden asks that quiet be maintained so all can enjoy the peace and tranquility.

The Wiesbaden Hot Springs Spa and Lodge offers European style and ambiance.

Miners tunneling in search of gold discovered a vapor cave. The first commercial spa on the site was Mother Buchanan's Bath House. The year was 1879, mining was booming, and there's loose talk that Mother Buchanan offered more than baths.

A recent archaeological study found the ruins of Chief Ouray's adobe home on the Wiesbaden property, uphill from the spa. He represented the seven Ute bands in nearly twenty years of negotiations with the U.S. government. Ouray died a year before an estimated twelve hundred Utes were removed from the Uncompahgre Valley at gunpoint in 1881. Ouray had a home in Montrose but used the adobe residence in Ouray for meetings with army officers and leaders of other Indian nations in his attempt to secure a permanent home for his tribe as treaty after treaty was broken.

Ouray, accused during his life of being a traitor to his people for seeking compromise instead of blood, took on an impossible task, for which he was uniquely qualified. He was born in New Mexico and grew up speaking Spanish and going to Catholic Mass. He also watched U.S. troops triumph in the Mexican-American War in 1846 and retaliate after the Taos revolt in 1847. He learned Ute from his mother, Apache from his father, and picked up English as well. Ouray moved to Colorado in 1850 and became a respected Ute leader.

Although successive treaties gave miners and cities and settlers thousands of acres they already occupied in western Colorado, Ouray retained a clear vision of the gruesome alternative. In the interest of peace, he dressed in a suit and tie, and his wife, Chipeta, served tea from a silver tea service. To urge the Utes to adapt, he farmed and ranched near Montrose. In the end, the Utes were exiled. Ouray died a year before his people were moved to reservations in Colorado and Utah. In the last few years of his life, Ouray returned to traditional Ute dress and habits.

The gold and silver ore around Ouray sealed the Utes' fate, but mining at 10,000 feet broke hundreds of settlers' hearts and lives as well. The winters, the failures, and the filth sent many away and a fair number to the grave. A few, like Thomas Walsh, owner of the Camp Bird Mine, became rich beyond their wildest dreams.

From Alfred Castner King, an early visitor to Ouray:

> Wherever I wander, my spirit still dwells,
> In the silvery San Juan with its streamlets and dells;
> Whose mountainous summits, so rugged and high,
> With their pinnacles pierce the ethereal sky;
> . . . Surrounded by mountains, majestic and gray,
> Which smile from their heights on the Town of Ouray.

In the 1920s, Dr. C. V. Bates opened a hospital on the spa site. Later, a dentist bought the motel, ran the springs as a spa, and practiced dentistry in a room off the lodge.

Today, The Wiesbaden is open to the public. It offers aromatherapy, massage, Austrian mud wraps, acupressure, and facials. Smoking and pets aren't allowed on the premises.

The view from the outdoor swimming pool is of alplike summits to the east and a stone-work tower surrounding a church bell to the west. The water temperature is about 100 degrees.

All the facilities are immaculate, including the vapor caves and pools. In a vapor chamber next to the springs, Linda has set semi-precious stones around the fixtures and plumbed another spring so that it flows over a rock face as a waterfall. The grounds are nicely landscaped and planted with hundreds of alpine flowers. Each of the dozen rooms, suites, and cabins is unique.

"The elegance, comfort and spirituality are all the essence of the Wiesbaden," says Linda, who matches the hummingbirds by being in constant motion.

Box Canyon Lodge and Hot Springs

45 3rd Avenue
Ouray 81421
(970) 325-4981
www.boxcanyonouray.com
Registered guests only; lodging; credit cards accepted
Where: From Main Street (U.S. 550) in Ouray, turn west onto 3rd
Avenue. Drive for 2 blocks. The Box Canyon Lodge is on the south
side of the street at the end of the second block on Ouray's south
side. See map, page 86.

This is a bird-watcher's hot springs paradise. The springs feed
into four wood tubs on redwood decks that terrace a hillside.
There's a 360-degree view of the surrounding mountains and
dozens of birds enticed by feeders. Frequent visitors include chick-
adees, grosbeaks galore, finches, hummingbirds, juncos, blue jays
that match the sky in color, and an occasional western tanager.

Use of the tubs is limited to guests, who can watch the sun
set over town and then enjoy the moonrise. The backdrop is
dramatic—the 13,000-foot peaks of the San Juan Mountains that
surround Ouray like a mighty legion. On a snowy night after cross-
country or downhill skiing in Telluride, each tub is a space mod-
ule that takes the soaker past Ouray's twinkling lights into the
historic mining town's lively past or into the twenty-first century
or up into the star systems above. The 4-feet high, 5-feet-in-
diameter tubs are vintage casks with wooden benches, each seat-
ing five people. Hydrojets shoot 103- to 108-degree water into the
tubs, bestowing the effervescence of champagne.

The Box Canyon springs have worn a host of hats to match
the fashions of many eras, from a simple bathhouse in the early
days to an exclusive sanitarium in 1925 run by Richard and
Bessie Cogar. "Ponce de Leon searched in the wrong section of the
country for the fountain of eternal youth," wrote one pleased

An early stereograph demonstrates why it's called Box Canyon. (Photograph courtesy Colorado Historical Society)

patient. "He should have come here and his dream would have been realized."

The name changed to Sweet Skin Sanitarium in 1929. By the end of World War II the springs had sprouted a motel for those seeking the rejuvenating powers of the water. Today some guests find the water so soothing that they take it home and reheat it for treatment of achy joints and muscles, says co-owner Barbara Uhles.

The springs hit 155 degrees in temperature, and the surplus heat heats the rooms as well as the hot water used for the sinks and bathtubs. The lodge offers rooms and suites, some with kitchens and some with fireplaces. A few open onto the hot tubs.

A short walk from the Box Canyon Lodge is the *real* Box Canyon and falls, which is a city park. To enter by car, there's an entrance south of town, off U.S. 550 going toward Silverton. A large sign directs drivers to turn right and cross a bridge into a parking lot. For hikers, the woodsy trail that starts 1 block west of the Box Canyon Lodge leads into a labyrinth of black rock walls with the sound of Canyon Creek below. Centuries of water flows have smoothed the rock. The trail leads through dark chambers, mists, patches of white sand beach, over a hanging bridge, up a walkway anchored to the rock wall, and past the waterfalls. The canyon is a place of roaring water, austere rock towers, and a sliver of sky up above.

Twin Peaks Motel

125 3rd Avenue
Ouray 81427
(970) 325-4427
www.subee.com/spa/home.html
Registered guests only; lodging; credit cards accepted
Where: Located on Ouray's south side, 1 block west of U.S. 550 (Main Street). From Main Street, turn west on 3rd Avenue and drive 1-1/2 blocks. The Twin Peaks is on the south side of the street. See map, page 86.

People still pull into the parking lot, jump out of the car, and take pictures of themselves in front of the sign that reads "Twin Peaks." "When the show was running on television, you couldn't keep pens and stationery," says Wendy Bazin, one of the owners of the motel.

The Twin Peaks is a Best Western lodge with an American Automobile Association four-diamond rating. Only registered guests can use the outdoor and indoor pools. The Twin Peaks is open six months a year, April through October. It's located next door to the Box Canyon Lodge.

The hotel occupies half of the original property of Richard and Bessie Cogar's sanitarium from the 1920s and is next door to the Box Canyon Lodge. In the old days, men's and women's tubs were separated for the sake of modesty. Today, Twin Peaks' outdoor pool is ringed by towering peaks and forest. The pool is maintained at about 82 degrees, and the outdoor soaking pool, complete with waterfall, is about 106 degrees. There are chairs and a deck for sunbathing.

The indoor pool is inside an A-frame with big windows. The 5-foot by 12-foot tub is a fiberglass shell with air jets that effervesce the water. The blue Mexican tile floor picks up the color of the sky.

The outdoor pool at Twin Peaks Motel, below the dramatic San Juan Mountains.

South on Main Street, or U.S. 550, the Million Dollar Highway starts. In the mining era that started in the 1880s and lasted into the 1920s, the road over 11,108-foot Red Mountain Pass and 10,901-foot Molas Divide Pass cost $1 million to engineer, blast, and smooth. That road, now U.S. 550, is paved, but for long stretches there are no guardrails on multiple hairpin turns. A straight drop down the cliffs starts a few feet from the yellow border line.

If that's not enough excitement, Twin Peaks rents jeeps for exploring the unpaved passes, abandoned mines, and high country above the treeline.

4UR Guest Ranch

P.O. Box 340
Creede 81130
(719) 658-2202
Registered guests only, with a one-week minimum stay; credit cards accepted
Where: From U.S. 160 near the town of South Fork, take Colorado 149 north 14 miles to the town of Wagon Wheel Gap. About a half-mile past the town, turn west (left) at the 4UR Guest Ranch sign, cross the bridge, and follow the gravel road for less than a mile to the ranch buildings.

F ishing is the specialty here, not soaking. The 4UR is an angler's resort ranch. Browns, rainbows, and native cutthroats dance in the Rio Grande River headwaters. There's also swimming, trap-shooting, rafting, riding, and hiking, for guests only.

Every summer a few hot springs devotees will ignore the four no-trespassing signs leading to the 4UR and arrive at the door, pleading to be allowed a dip. Alas, the rules prevail and unregistered visitors are politely turned away.

Julia Child, former president Dwight D. Eisenhower, and Walt Disney have fished at the 5,000-acre resort ranch renowned for gourmet meals.

Fishing did take second billing to the hot springs with the Utes. Settlers later said the Utes called the hot springs "Little Medicine." That distinguished the area from Pagosa Springs, which settlers said the Utes called "Big Medicine." A foot trail connected the two distant springs before miners and settlers arrived.

When the first resort was built there during the spa era, the hot springs eclipsed fishing. In the 1870s, Lake City miners borrowed English money to build curative pools for invalids and arthritic miners. The resort was also a stop on the European spa circuit, a

4UR Guest Ranch

to Creede

Wagon Wheel Gap

4UR GUEST RANCH

Rio

149

Grande

Rio Grande

South Fork

to Alamosa

RIO GRANDE

Fork

160

NATIONAL FOREST

South

Wolf Creek Pass

to Pagosa Springs

NORTH

The outdoor pool at 4UR Guest Ranch.

worldwide network of mountain getaways that offered baths, mineral water, and other tonics. At the resort, called Wagon Wheel Gap, there was a comfortable hotel with thirty pools of bubbling water that ranged in temperature from icy to near boiling.

The name Wagon Wheel Gap originated in the 1860s, when miners found a wagon wheel in the area and presumed it was left by John Frémont's expedition, which ended in starvation in 1848. More likely, the wheel was left by George Baker on a later journey. But the name stuck. Baker's party went on to found the town of Silverton.

History dropped by the neighborhood again in the late 1870s with railroad tycoon General William Palmer, best known for putting Colorado Springs, Durango, and Alamosa on the map by building rail service. He bought the springs, built a complete resort, and operated a highbrow guest ranch. Patrons enjoyed fine dining, good fishing, and the salubrious effects of the hot springs.

"I know of no place in Colorado where the fly-fisher will have better sport," wrote author Ernest Ingersoll, who came by in the late 1880s. Enchanted with the fish, Ingersoll also noted the springs' allure. "There are accounts of men brought here utterly helpless and full of agony from inflammatory rheumatism or neuralgia who in a week are able to walk about and help themselves, in a fortnight were strolling about the valley perfectly erect and comfortable and who in a month went to work."

There is also the tale of the wife of an early owner who bathed in the nude. Her servant accompanied her to the springs, using an umbrella to protect the mistress of the manor from the stares of cowboys.

In 1889, five thousand pounds of trout were reportedly caught in the river. A 1905 brochure spoke of the "Resort and Fishing Place." A 1901 letter to the editor of the *Denver Times* exhorted readers to "Away with your Newport! Away with your Manitou! Away with your ocean breezes and delicious salt air! Give us some Wagon Wheel Gap."

Meanwhile, back on the ranch, sixteen families had homesteaded the valley, managing to sustain life against barbaric winters and brief growing seasons. Many of the settlers' descendants still live in the area, and family ties enhance the community closeness.

In 1904, General Palmer embarked on an ambitious $25,000 renovation that included the elegant stone bathhouse that still stands. A casino was in place by 1908, along with a dance floor. Each of the main springs had a name: Hot Soda, Hot Saline, Cold Lithia, and Hot Sulfur.

The current managers carry on Palmer's tradition of genteel hospitality and lavish meals.

The largest spring is located on the edge of the property and ringed with a cement retaining pool fashionably adorned with cattle skulls and clusters of crystals. The swimming pool, located near the main ranch house, has a large deck, changing rooms, and a hot tub, mere adjuncts to the fishing.

Dunton Hot Springs

P.O. Box 3582
Telluride 81435
(970) 728-4840
Check with telephone information for new number
Private development; limited rental to groups
Where: There's a short way to Dunton and a long way. Both routes start from Colorado 145 between Telluride and Dolores and use the Dunton Road (FS 535), a mostly unpaved 37-mile road off Colorado 145. The shorter route, which is usually impassable in the winter, starts on Colorado 145 about 15 miles south of Telluride. Turn west from Colorado 145 at the sign for Dunton and follow the steep and winding Dunton Road for about 15 miles to the hamlet of Dunton. Four-wheel-drive is recommended. The year-round route starts farther south on Colorado 145 just west of the town of Stoner and about 15 miles northwest of Dolores. From Colorado 145, turn north onto the Dunton Road and follow the route about 22 miles to Dunton.

A hot springs reincarnation. Like a phoenix, the Dunton hot springs are rising from years of vandalism, abandonment, and decay into a private development. The "concept" is still evolving, so the public may or may not be welcome to visit the final product.

Telluride real estate developers Bernt Kuhlmann and Christoph Henkel first visited Dunton in the dead of winter in 1994, reaching the remote ramshackle buildings on snowshoes. Within fifteen minutes on that snowy January day, the two decided to buy the 187-acre property for $1.1 million. During the two-hour drive out, they developed the guiding concept for Dunton's new life, that of a recreated Colorado mountain town of between 1820 and 1840.

At Dunton Hot Springs, even the old bathhouse has been reconstructed.

Dunton Hot Springs

"That period before 1840 was an innocent time," says Bernt, a former Los Angeles screenwriter. "It was before the Indian wars, before the gold rush. It was the frontier. It was the West that we as children in Europe grew up with."

When Christoph Henkel and Bernt Kuhlmann first visited Dunton in 1994, the town and the hot springs had been abandoned for more than a decade. The drinking water had been contaminated in the 1980s and the state health department closed the hot springs.

By the fall of 1999, the makings of a town had emerged. Bernt, an Austrian, and Christoph, a German, had bought antique cabins, barns, and farmhouses in several western states and moved them to Dunton, log by log, for reassembly in coming years. Renovation of the saloon and several cabins are nearly finished.

The hot springs are likewise reborn. A tepee raised on a red-wood deck covers the hot spring's source. The pool, sunken below the deck and reached by a simple wooden ladder, is about 3-1/2 feet deep with a bench along one side for long soaks. The water temperature is about 106 degrees. The lighting through the tepee is warm sepia, the air is tropical, and the ambiance is serene.

The water flows into the original pool located in the old bath-house, which has been reconstructed from materials salvaged from the original building. Light pours in through cracks in the wood siding, the roof, and the floor. The pool is 12 feet by 8 feet, and 4 feet deep. Against the wall leans an old mirror with a bar of soap and an old razor, as if waiting for a miner, a homesteader, or an outlaw motorcycle rider.

Dunton was established in 1885, when miners were staking claims on the West Dolores River, and a Horatio Dunton filed on the town site. Local lore says that cabins lined the river for miles and about three hundred people lived in log homes, drank at a number of saloons, and traded at the stores. Legend says Butch Cassidy hid in Dunton after robbing the Telluride Bank in 1889. The old bar located in the renovated saloon has hundreds of names and initials carved into the wood, including Butch's.

Miners came from miles away to soak at the bathhouse, but by 1918 the gold was gone. That's the year Joe and Dominica Roscio bought the property, started a dude ranch, and converted two of the old saloons into a dance hall. "They found that the hot water was the real gold mine," says Bernt. The Roscios sold out in 1980 to a group of New York investors, who tried to resell the property without success until Christoph and Bernt came on the scene.

Under its various owners Dunton was always free spirited, and clothing was rare at the springs. From three to a dozen people lived in town, and the saloon drew customers from many miles. In the 1960s, waves of hippies, motorcycle gypsies, and musicians came and stayed for varying lengths of time. Sometimes there were fights, sometimes soaking in the springs smoothed the conflicts. When the Roscios ordered a group of bikers out in 1977, they burned a couple of cabins as a way of saying good-bye, then they left.

Now there is the Dunton Concept.

Dunton will be modeled on the idealistic landscapes of George Catlin, Karl Bodmer, and Jacob Miller, whose enormous oil paintings of elysian meadows beneath the West's regal mountain peaks captured Europe's imagination in the late 1800s. Seventeen home sites, of 4 to 12 acres each, started at $200,000. While Rancho Dolores at Dunton owners will fish and hunt, walk and explore nature, there will be no golf or daily shoot-outs. Residents will be encouraged to buy tepees to use as guest houses.

Bernt and Christoph haven't decided whether any part of Dunton would be available to the general public. Walk-ins are definitely out, but groups may be able to rent the town—complete with saloon and dance hall—and hot pools for a weekend. Inquire before visiting.

Mineral Hot Springs Spa

28640 County Road 58EE
Moffat 81143
(719) 256-4328
Open to the public
Where: On Colorado Highway 17, 32 miles south of Salida and 50 miles north of Alamosa. Highway 17 runs parallel to Highway 285. On the east side of the road, marked by whitewashed building.

The view from the pools at Mineral Hot Springs, shielded from the wind by plexi glass, is a living diorama of a thriving high mountain desert backed by 14,000 foot peaks. Owls head out to hunt at dusk and court in the sky during February. Jackrabbits munch, ever alert for winged predators. Antelope wander by. And sometimes the population of songbirds gets so raucous that any human chatter is lost in the noise. At dusk, when the roiling clouds turn as golden as the October desert floor, it's evocative of Tibet.

Serenity. Mediative quiet. The scent of herbs. A soft refrain of flute music. Simple elegant architecture, somewhere between southwest and Morocco and Cape Cod.

Summer weekends fill with truth seekers from Crestone and weekender getaway wanderers from Denver, Boulder, and Colorado Springs.

After nearly twenty-five years of closure, the Mineral Hot Springs reopened in 1995, the work of Victor Summers and Lotus McElfish. Earlier, the Summers helped transform Glen Ivy Hot Springs in California into a resort. When they were traveling in Colorado looking for a new project, a friend in Crestone told them about Mineral.

Local lore tells of thousands of Ute artifacts found at the springs, indicating heavy use by the original inhabitants. In 1880, the year the Utes were confined to reservations, homesteader Sylvester Jenks claimed the newly available springs. And about the same time, a coal company opened the Orient Mine about 6 miles away. By 1892, a town had sprouted to serve the visitors who came by train over Poncha Pass to savor the hot pools, mud room, and lodgings.

Mineral's glory days arrived in the early 1900s. The Robert Dunshee family, who had made their money by brokering real estate deals in the area, changed the name to Mineral Hot Springs. The town was plotted, thirty-seven springs were counted, postal service was arranged, the dance hall drew railroaders, farmers, and store keepers for dozens of miles. And the spring's offerings were expanded to include an enclosed pool, bathhouse, and cottage camp. When Dunshee died, a series of other owners took over until the 1960s when the town was abandoned. At some point, the elevated redwood tank that held water for the train and marked the springs in the otherwise flat area was stolen.

In the 1980s, the North Chamberlain Swine Unit moved in, setting up 125 train box cars to house the pigs. The springs' heat warmed the swine. After the pig farm went out of business, Mineral languished for years, until Summers and McElfish came along.

The place has come a long way and Summers and McElfish have an album of construction photos to prove it. Anyone considering a hot springs rehab should take a peek before plunking down earnest money. The husband and wife team transformed a highway eyesore into a place of beauty and solace.

While Mineral Hot Springs is the only building for miles, Lady Bird Johnson and the Highway Beautification Act, which put the kibosh on billboards, left a legacy of challenges for advertising. Summers and McElfish adopted a stretch of Highway 285 before the Highway 17 cutoff so the spa's name is on the north access and they painted the old gas station white with black block letters that are highly visible in the otherwise unpopulated area.

The springs rush from the earth at 145 degrees Fahrenheit, and the couple keeps the pools at 103 to 108 degrees and don't add chemicals because the water replaces itself each day. The

Serenity surrounds Mineral Hot Springs.

changing rooms and lockers sparkle. The wooden decks are smooth, and the temple-like walls are whitewashed and gleaming.

In the private baths, blends of camomile, orange peel, rose petal, and lavender can enhance the soothing warm water. Thoughtfully designed head rests add further comfort in the private, two-person soaking tank. The sauna is aspen-paneled and offers a view of the Sangre de Cristo Mountains.

In the outdoor Tower Pool, surrounded by white columns and decking, the freshly scrubbed white tile tub outside drops down so arms, shoulders, and necks submerge. There are two other soaking pools, which measure about 10 feet by 10 feet, offering a light pollution-free desertscape perfect for viewing the rising moon, starry dances, roaming fogs, sudden rains, and rainbows.

There's no diving board or kids' pool. Youngsters prefer Splashland, open only in the summer; the Salida Pool; and the Sand Dunes Swimming Pool, open year-round.

And Mineral has a sense of fun.

In March, the spa hosts the Flamingo Festival, a witty parody of the valley's crane festival which welcomes the stopover of whooping cranes near Monte Vista on their annual migration north from Mexico.

Not everyone gets the gentle joke. Flamingos don't migrate through Colorado excepted when stuffed and hauled on moving trucks. But a flock of wooden, metal, plastic, and otherwise ersatz flamingos does roost at Mineral for three weeks in March, the fevered pink enlivening the winterscape environs. Guests who donate to the flock receive a free pass for another soak.

Mineral Hot Springs has become popular with visitors to the San Luis Valley taking classes in healing arts, UFOs, spiritualism, and New Age teachings at Crestone, 10 miles to the north. The influx of seekers soaking in the pools makes for enlightening conversations about past life regressions, comparative meditation techniques, and yoga for body or mind.

The unexplained lights hovering in the night sky date back to the 1950s. In the post-nuclear years of dating, couples would park atop hills, windshields pointed southeast, and reportedly catch glimpses of UFOs, brilliant and fast moving lights, and other mysterious objects. There's even talk of building an observation tower—only 10 feet tall—near Hooper.

With or without extraterrestrials, there's a lot to see: the Sand Dunes National Monument, the Alligator Farm, the old Catholic missions at tiny San Luis Valley towns, the Stations of the Cross sculptures at San Luis, and the Crane Festival at Monte Vista in March.

But at Mineral Hot Springs, the desert seasons at 7,700 feet elevation pass in the 200-degree view outside the glass-enclosed hot pools and decks. As the months pass, snow gives way to pale greens and purples of spring. Fierce, late spring snowstorms give way to pale gold light that turns the flat wet flakes into clusters of diamonds on the dried grasses. The longer days and warmer nights foster wildflowers that trade off the starring role throughout the summer. Sudden thunderstorms fire their fury on the land and roil on down the valley, leaving rainbows and the scent of sage in their wake.

And the nights of galaxies above climax in mid-August when hosts of shooting stars rain across the sky. It's a show that's drawn lookers for centuries to marvel at the celestial show from the balmy, odorless waters.

Valley View Hot Springs

County Road GG
P.O. Box 175
Villa Grove 81155
(719) 256-4315
www.vvhs.com/soak
Members only on weekends; clothing optional; lodging; credit cards accepted
Where: In the San Luis Valley, about 27 miles south of Poncha Springs on U.S. 285. About 4-1/2 miles south of Villa Grove, at the junction of U.S. 285 and Colorado 17, turn left (east) on County Road GG, a gravel road. Follow CR GG about 7-1/2 miles to Valley View's entrance.

On a clear day, hundreds of snowcapped summits in Colorado and New Mexico frame a 200-mile stretch of the San Luis Valley for a drop-dead view. Valley View Hot Springs is located at an elevation of 8,700 feet on the toes of the Sangre de Cristo Mountains and overlooks the Continental Divide. To the far south is Great Sand Dunes National Monument. To the north, the low flat valley is bordered by the Himalayan-like scenery of two towering mountain ranges—the Sangres and the La Garita Mountains.

That view dominates the landscape around the four natural ponds and the sandy-bottomed communal pool tucked into the hillside. The new swimming pool and adjacent children's wading pool also looks out on the valley. There's another pool inside the wood-burning sauna. None of the pools are chemically treated.

"It's like the Old West. It's the land that time forgot," says Neil Seitz, who owns the remote springs with his wife, Terry.

The San Luis Valley, where the Spanish first settled in Colorado, has little of the development, air pollution, or urbanization that other mountain communities have experienced. Spanish land

Kids of all ages enjoy Valley View Hot Springs.

grants kept large tracts of land intact and launched a few mighty dreams for the region.

The Spanish conquistadors and explorers in the 1500s and 1600s named the Sangre de Cristo Mountains for the "blood of Christ." Dozens of San Luis Valley towns, rivers, and peaks also bear names bestowed by the early Spanish expeditions, which sought gold in vain.

To secure the land throughout southwestern Colorado and northern New Mexico in the 1800s, Spanish kings awarded loyalist nobles with enormous land grants. In Spain at that time, only the oldest son inherited the family wealth, and no other land was available. The land grants were a miracle—new land was created. In exchange, the recipients swore to create permanent settlements of loyal Spanish citizens.

The Sangre de Cristo Grant of 1843 included most of the San Luis Valley. The Utes, who didn't recognize the right of the Spanish king to give their homeland away, made settlement difficult until the 1880s, when they were removed by the U.S. Army.

Alamosa Area

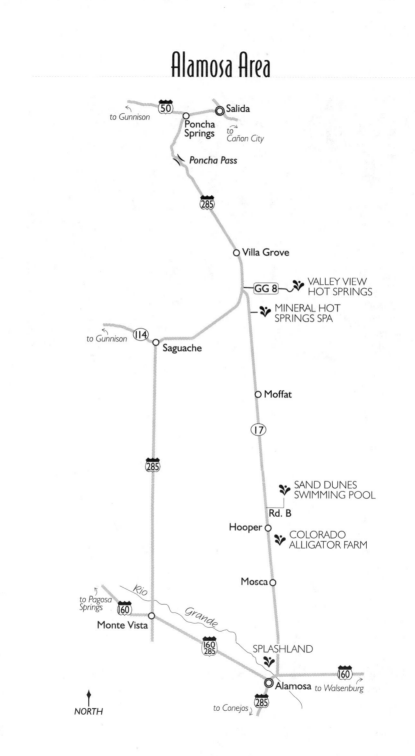

The valley remains a place of big dreams. The late Malcolm Forbes bought part of the Trinchera Land Grant near Great Sand Dunes National Monument. He kept part as a ranch and planned a housing development. Ads in the international editions of *Forbes* and *Time* magazines have led to the sale of most of the lots. The Forbes family regularly visits the ranch, now known as the Forbes Trinchera.

The Spanish Catholics in the Valley's southern end, past Alamosa, observe two-hundred-year-old rituals at Christmas, Easter, and other religious holidays. On Good Friday, hundreds gather at the Stations of the Cross Shrine, *La Mesa de la Pieda y de la Misericorda*, in San Luis to reenact Christ's journey to the crucifixion. At each of the "stations" or stops that Christ made is a life-sized bronze sculpture of Jesus' agony. At the top of the mesa, sculptor Huberto Maestas created The Resurrection.

And near Crestone in the northern valley, Canadian industrialist Maurice Strong bought part of another land grant and endowed a Tibetan monastery, a Hindu ashram, Benedictine monks, Carmelite nuns, and other religious groups. He gave them land and support to establish religious settlements. He also built a conference center that draws world political, business, and spiritual leaders.

Overlooking the valley in all its diversity is the Valley View Hot Springs—idyllic, scenic, and clothing-optional. In the 1960s, that nomadic, colorful, and rebellious tribe known as hippies discovered the abandoned hot springs and created a bare-bottom haven. They're still coming. "We have some of the same people coming as we did twenty years ago," says Neil. "They have children or their children have children."

Most bathers opt against swimsuits. Some spend the day working on full-body tans. Others drop their clothing poolside. Those in bathing suits are as welcome as the unclothed. And nearly everyone dresses in the evening when the temperatures plunge.

"Naturist," not nudist, is the term of choice. Naturists, according to the Naturist Society, enjoy getting naked, protect the environment, differentiate between nakedness and sexuality, and are nonevangelical. The philosophy works well at Valley View, where only members and their guests are permitted on weekends. The naturist rules also apply during the week, when it's open to the public. There are rustic cabins, rooms, and camping, all with a communal rest room. The waiting list for membership is long. The resort caters primarily to families with children.

The setting is primeval. Deer wander up to the pool and drink while bathers watch. The natural hot pools are draped with filaments of warmwater plants. The pools are dispersed, and the only sounds are wind, trees, and birds. A full moon on a clear night illuminates the valley like an Ansel Adams landscape—art and nature fused in incandescent beauty.

Most of the bathers live along Colorado's Front Range, which stretches from Pueblo in the south to Fort Collins in the north. Bathers from afar include visitors from the international meeting facilities at Crestone, guests at the Forbes ranch, bird-watchers, and students from Colorado College wanting to try out naturism.

The quantity of arrowheads found around the springs tells of its extensive use by early Native Americans. After the Utes were removed to reservations in 1881, Valley View became a resort.

In the early 1900s John Everson ran the operation and catered to iron-ore miners from the neighboring Orient Mine. The miners used the springs through the 1930s. The Seitz property includes the mine and part of a narrow-gauge rail route. The springs, along with Everson's store and other buildings, were abandoned after World War II and remained vacant until the 1960s, when hippies set up housekeeping at the site.

Neil was hired as caretaker by John Everson's grandson Roy in 1975 and rousted cowboys bent on teaching hippies country manners. Neil converted drunken brawls into peaceable gatherings. He carried a shotgun and made citizens arrests. He bought the springs in 1979.

Until 1980, Valley View's only phone had an unlisted number. The cabins still don't have separate phones. They don't advertise and there's no sign on the highway. Guest numbers rarely top eighty on a busy summer weekend, when only members are allowed, and rarely hit forty on winter weekends.

Neil, a man of many talents, developed a hydroelectric system that heats and lights the entire resort. "We're kind of high-tech funky laid-back," he says.

Sand Dunes Swimming Pool

(Also Known as Hooper Pool)
1991 Colorado Road 63
Hooper 81136
(719) 378-2807
Open to the public; year round; half days December and January;
major credit cards accepted
Where: On Highway 17 between Salida and Alamosa. From the
town of Hooper, about midway, go north on 17 for 1 mile. On the
right or east side of the road, look for the "Road B" sign and turn
right. Continue east on the gravel road for about 1.5 miles. At the
T in the road, take a left onto Road 63. Drive north for about 1
mile. The pool is on your left.

Who says there's not enough for kids to do in the San Luis
Valley? Certainly not anyone who has stopped at the newly
reopened Sand Dunes Swimming Pool, known locally as the
Hooper Pool.

Not that the Alligator Farm and the Splashland Pool weren't
enough entertainment to enliven the kidlets on the drive to and
from the Great Sand Dunes National Monument. The Sand Dunes
Pool is a bonus because the water is warm and it's open all year.
And while there are no alligators, there's a stream of talapia, a pha-
lanx of barbecue grills, volleyball and basketball courts, and a
snack bar with 75 cent hot dogs—at least as of 1999.

The owners, Ed and Sharie Harmon, created a family-style hot
spring because they have five children themselves. The Harmons
are also organic farmers, producing hydroponic tomatoes and English cucumbers in the greenhouses. They lease out the rest of the
family farm for grain and carrots.

Until the Harmons reopened the pool in 1995, the oasis had
been closed to the public for twenty years. Both the Harmons grew

up in the area and remember the wooden slat fence around the warm pool and dressing rooms.

The pool tale starts with oil exploration in the 1930s when drilling went down 5,000 feet down without striking oil. However, hot water poured from the hole and the Hooper Swimming Pool had its first incarnation. The hot springs at Salida, Mineral, Valley View, and Splashland all come from the same geological fault. At the tap, the water is 118 degrees Fahrenheit. The first owner closed it down in 1978. In the 1980s, catfish skulked in the pools. And in the 1990s, a New York investment group sought out the Harmons, who were farming nearby, as prospective buyers.

"It was a meant to be kind of thing," said Sharie Harmon.

The Harmons rebuilt the pool, put up the adobe wall, added the large covered patio, and leased out their farm. Their older daughters lifeguard, teach swimming, run the snack bar, and help operate the pool. The younger children haul frozen food for the snack bar, patrol the walkways for trash, and keep an eye on the little kids.

In the years the pool was officially closed, it was unofficially used by locals after a night on the town. They'd climb the fence and shed their clothes before frolicking in the algae and warm water. For the first few years, the Harmons and the resident manager had a few nighttime visitors who had high hopes of reliberating the hot springs.

The Sand Dunes Pool is family with a capital "P" on parents. No kid drop-offs for youngsters under fourteen. There are lifeguards on summer afternoons, but the Harmons require children to come with parents, grandparents, or caretakers. Safety was the reason, but as a result, the Sand Dunes Pool is a bit quieter than your average swimming pool.

The pool temperature is 98 to 100 degrees in the summer and about 103 in the winter. While the summer is lively with day care groups, school kids, and families, the winter crowd is just as numerous if a bit more mature with lap swimmers, older folks soaking up the heat, and off-season travelers en route to Taos and Santa Fe, or Denver and Boulder. Convoys of students from Adams State

Farmer-fashioned fountain.

College in Alamosa take study breaks here. When it's snowing or the temperature drops below 15 degrees, business picks up.

For adults, the farmer-fashioned shower that pours hot water from 10 feet above the pool is a welcome massage for the neck, arms, and shoulders. The fountain is welded from irrigation sprinkler parts and is a tribute to the ingenuity of farmers.

"We wanted to create a metal palm tree, but we haven't gotten around to it yet," said Sharie. "Even without the palm fronds, the water feels so good on your back."

Unlike the water theme parks in the metropolitan area, the Sand Dunes Pool charges prices kids can afford for food and floats. Foam noodles and kick boards rent for about 50 cents. A life-size alligator runs $1.

"We wanted to encourage them to have a little more fun," said Sharie. "Most pools won't allow water toys, but the kids love them."

Sharie said she felt guilty when they had to raise the price of hot dogs from 50 cents.

"I hate to see the kids just buy candy because that's all they have money for. This way, they buy lots of hot dogs. We had a family from New York that couldn't believe their lunches were less than $10. We're not out to make a fortune."

Thoughts of water slides, private hot tubs, and fishing ponds intrigue the Harmons. During the winter and each spring, they add something new to the area.

"Who knows what all will be here in five or ten years," said Sharie.

The Harmons, like nearly everyone else in the San Luis Valley, are nervous about plans to "mine" the ground water under the valley floor and pipe the water to the Denver metropolitan area. The courts and voters have rebuffed the attempts for twenty years. But with the develop craze in water-short Douglas County and Aurora, another scheme will arise.

"A deep well in the wrong place could end this whole place," she said.

The Sand Dunes Pool closes for ten days in March and April for cleaning, painting, and remodeling. The hours run from 1 P.M. to 8 P.M. in December and January. And, the pool closes on Thursday for draining and cleaning. But otherwise it's open from 10 A.M. until 10 P.M.

There's only a little chlorine in the water. The daily flow through keeps the pool clean and more chemicals would hurt the talapia and gambuzzies, which were added to help control the mosquitoes. Organic tomatoes and hot springs pools and UFOs.

Ever since the 1950s, Hooperites have spotted rapidly moving lights in the skies and compared sightings. Even sheriff's deputies claim to have seen UFOs, which do bring hundreds of people hoping for a close encounter of any kind in the San Luis Valley.

Colorado Alligator Farm

P.O. Box 1052
Alamosa 81101
(719) 589-3032
www.gatorfarm.com
Visitors welcome; credit cards accepted
Where: In the San Luis Valley where Colorado 17 branches off from U.S. 285 going south to Alamosa. Drive south about 30 miles on Colorado 17 past Moffat and Hooper. Turn east (left) at the sign for the Colorado Alligator Farm. Follow the signs for about 2 blocks to the greenhouse buildings and the parking lot. See map, page 120.

Not all Colorado hot springs are for humans. In a high-mountain desert ringed by 14,000-foot peaks, immigrant Florida alligators bask in the sun, ever watchful for a snack. Every yawn reveals an army of teeth. Hours of torpor end in a split-second dash across the pool. Truly a worthy roadside attraction.

The geothermal well near Hooper married the ecological odd couple of 83 alligators and 1.5 million North African tilapia—a piscine delicacy popular for its sweet nonfishy flavor—and a Rocky Mountain valley. The marriage arrangements started with Erwin and Lynne Young raising catfish in Lubbock, Texas, and using the tropical tilapia to clean the water. The tilapia grew faster than the catfish and brought more money at the market because of their exotic origins and flavor. But the new venture was thwarted when the tilapia began to die in the mild Texas winters.

The solution to the Youngs' fish habitat quandary was far afield in Colorado's San Luis Valley, where the couple bought the 87-degree well in 1977. The Youngs' own hybrid species, Rocky Mountain white tilapia, prospered in the high-altitude waters. Most are shipped live to markets across the country, but the

Just a few of the contented residents of Colorado Alligator Farm.

Youngs recruited the bevy of alligators to feast on the fragrant by-products of processing about five thousand pounds of fish a year.

The toothy adult gators evolved into a tourist attraction. Ever grinning, they reside in a city-block-sized pool of warm water and have adapted to the snowy Rocky Mountain winters by sleeping a lot. Weighing in at three hundred to six hundred pounds, the 6- to 10-foot-long alligators have hearty appetites far exceeding the available supply of fish parts. Erwin supplements their diet with commercial packaged alligator food and protein pellets.

To reduce costs, Erwin once tried throwing in dead livestock from local ranches but found that the alligator pack then became too aggressive. On days when no dead cow appeared, the gators attacked other gators. A few of the fellows are missing legs from the days of cannibalistic carnage. One lost his tail in an unfriendly frenzy.

Visitors can buy a bucket of alligator food for $1. Just about any time of day, the gang of gators can put on a good show when fed. The sounds of jaws snapping, tails thrashing in the water, and guttural growls add a vivid sound element to home videos.

The Alligator Farm's brochure explains what alligators eat: Whatever they want. Swamp studies have found sticks, stones, shotgun shells, cigarettes, fishing lures, dog tags, cans, and plastic cigar holders in the guts of gators. In their native home swamps, alligators prefer fish, snails, amphibians, birds, snakes, turtles, insects, and crayfish.

The handout also includes Alligator Awfuls: What do you call an alligator detective? An investi-gator. What do alligators do when they lose their tails? Go to a retail store. What do you say to a sick alligator? See you later illigator. And so on . . .

The water that cradles tilapia and warms alligator blood goes on to create a wetland. Canadian geese, pheasants, eagles, great blue herons, and other bird species flock to the acres of pools, along with bird-watchers and hikers. A strange marriage made in a bizarre anteroom of warm water heaven.

Splashland

P.O. Box 972
Alamosa 81101
(719) 589-6307
Open to the public; summer only; credit cards not accepted
Where: On Colorado 17 about 1 mile north of Alamosa. Splashland is the adobe-colored building on the west side of the highway. See map, page 120.

"You can do it Nicole," says a girl underneath the high board. "Jump. Jump. Jump," chant the other swimmers. And Nicole takes the big leap. High drama at Splashland, repeated daily between Memorial Day and Labor Day for over forty years.

Located outside of Alamosa in a farming area, Splashland offers a big swimming pool and a kiddie wading pool, locker rooms, and food prices of the 1950s. There's rock and roll on the public address system and the lifeguards seem to know everyone's name. And there are lots of signs, including: "No hanging on the signs."

It looks like an adobe fortress from a distance, but it's the summer home for kids from a dozen San Luis Valley communities. It's also a vacationing kids' oasis after Great Sand Dunes National Monument, the Monte Vista National Wildlife Refuge, or the drive between Denver and Santa Fe.

It was Lloyd Jones's idea. The Alamosa rancher decided he'd heard about too many children who drowned in irrigation ditches and the Rio Grande River. He wanted a place where they could learn to swim and could swim safely. He happened to own a piece of land with a warm artesian spring, and that's where he built the pool in 1955.

Lloyd ran the pool for more than thirty years, continued ranching, and decided in the late 1980s that he'd done his part. He

Splashland has been providing summer fun to Alamosa residents for more than forty years.

offered to sell the pool to the city of Alamosa, but the city wasn't interested. Lloyd had other things to do and planned to close the pool. Judy Crisco had small children and didn't want to see it closed. She and other concerned citizens organized a pledge campaign and raised enough for a down payment. Children donated money, people bought lifetime memberships, local businesses donated money, as did the city and county. And another generation is learning to swim and dive.

On any given summer day there are school buses from summer programs in Crestone, La Veta, and Antonito. There are groups from Head Start, Colorado Migrant Services, and summer sports programs. With a donation of canned food for the Community Food Bank, July 4 and Labor Day are free of charge. There are early-morning laps for seniors and barbeques at night.

"Its more than recreation, it's a community resource," Judy says.

The big pool is 150 feet by 60 feet, and 10 feet deep. But it's built for kids—the shallow end lasts for 75 feet with only a 1-foot dropoff. The water is about 94 degrees. The kiddie pool is a toasty 85 degrees.

"Some days when it's really hot out, the refreshing part is getting *out* of the water," says Judy. But at 7,500 feet, the warmth is usually welcome.

Rainbow Hot Springs

**Weminuche Wilderness Area in the
San Juan National Forest**
No charge; clothing optional; primitive wilderness location
Where: From Pagosa Springs, take U.S. 160 northeast for 18 miles
to the sign for the West Fork Campground, which is on the west
side of the highway. The West Fork Campground is on the southwest side of Wolf Creek Pass. Take the West Fork Campground
road for 6.9 miles to the West Fork Trailhead. The last mile or so
of the road may be closed for construction. To get to the spring is
an 8- to 10-mile hike round-trip, depending on the road closures,
with a 1,200-foot elevation gain going in. It's difficult. Allow five
to eight hours for the round-trip hike.

You'll need a good soak, but you may have to stand in line for a
place in the pool.

The trail ends about 200 feet above the two terraced pools set
in the rock beside the river like small, perfect diamonds. With
sandy bottoms, the pools are waist-high when you are sitting. The
smaller pool is set up on the rock face in a sliver carved out of the
stone. With room for about three, it offers a nice river view and the
proper perspective for contemplating the fissure from which the
104-degree springs pour. For most people, it's too warm for long
periods of contemplation.

The lower pool, which seats about eight, is a hot-tubbers fantasy. The rock wall allows for temperature control, and smooth flat
rocks along the side are perfect for sitting while dangling sore feet
in the pool. A tiny pool to one side is perfect for solo bathing. And
it's a hop, skip, and a jump into the West Fork of the San Juan
River for a brisk cooldown. As with all public springs, the pools
change with the energy and building skills of the visitors.

Rainbow Hot Springs

RAINBOW HOT SPRINGS

Beaver Creek

West Fork San Juan

WEMINUCHE
WILDERNESS
AREA

Sheep Mtn.
(12,369)

to South Fork via
Wolf Creek Pass

Wolf Creek

Borns Lake

561

SAN JUAN

NATIONAL

FOREST

WEST FORK

FR 648

RD

Fall Creek

Treasure
Falls

River

160

NORTH

to Pagosa Springs

Rainbow Hot Springs—a delicious reward for the grueling hike in.

Horse trips come to the springs, as do hunters, folks on snow-shoes and on cross-country skis. For years the difficulty of fording the river controlled the crowds, but after a backpacker drowned, the U.S. Forest Service built two bridges and improved access.

At the end of the difficult hike up on an August Sunday, this intrepid hot springs seeker was astonished to find more than a dozen tents, three with barking dogs. There were another dozen tents outside the main camping area. As for most wilderness areas, the Forest Service doesn't require backcountry permits for campers at Rainbow Hot Springs.

Which is all to say that it's lovely, but don't count on anything like a pristine wilderness experience.

The trip in is grueling, a challenge for the hardiest hiker. The trail varies from a four-wheel-drive road to a 2-inch rock ledge. There's a steep section through scree (loose rock). And after the Weminuche Wilderness Area sign shortly after the residential area, signs are scarce, but horseback trips to the springs and hordes of hikers have left a fairly clear trail.

The first mile of trail, which starts at Born Lake, winds through a neighborhood of summer cabins. The owners have heavily embellished the forest with private-property signs and a wealth of signs for Rainbow Trail with arrows. Off to the left, the emerald lake beckons, surrounded by more "Private Property" signs.

In 1995 the hike was 10 miles because the road was closed two places below Born Lake. Homeowners, going to and fro while moving the portable "Closed" sign, admonished hikers about the dangers of the road ahead. Hikers tackling the extra miles noticed road work, but the road was passable. Of course, the closure did cut down significantly on traffic past residences.

At the end of the residential area, about a mile from the gate at Born Lake, the trail snakes through deep piney woods, aspen groves, banks of wildflowers, crowds of ferns, a throng of towering skunk cabbage, and across three bridges.

The second and third bridges are recent. For years, the river decided who reached the hot springs. Spring runoff, which sometimes lasts until August in high snowpack years, once dissuaded many hot springs seekers who chose not to ford a chest-high river of ice water. The river carried many of the foolhardy dozens of feet downstream.

At the bridges, the river smiles in deep blue pools, pale green shallows, and frothy white falls. Trout flutter in shady sand-bottomed sections. The trail and river entwine. Right after the last bridge there's a nasty half-mile of trail that shoots upward in a 15 and 20 percent grade, warning the traveler that the remaining 2 miles won't be a walk in the park. There are sections of muddy bogs, narrow goat trails along a rock face, and steep climbs. Although there's a net 1,000-foot elevation gain, there's enough up-and-down to convince hikers' calves that the gross gain is closer to 2,000 feet.

Since the early 1990s, teams of biologists have spent summer weeks and months in the Weminuche Wilderness searching for grizzlies. The last known grizzly in Colorado was killed decades ago by a hunting guide, and no grizzly has been spotted—officially—since. Bear-sighting stories abound, but the biologists have found no evidence, so far, of bears. But many are convinced the grizzly is alive and well somewhere in the thousands of acres of the Weminuche Wilderness. Prints in the sandy shores along the riverside report of deer, elk, and a variety of small furry wildlife with long nails.

The last mile seems the longest. At one point, the trail divides. The left fork is labeled Continental Divide, the right is Beaver Creek/Beaver Meadows. There's no mention of Rainbow Hot Springs. Take the left. Better still, you should pack a San Juan National Forest map.

No sign marks the springs, but the "tentopolis" with rock-rimmed fire circles says you're there.

The riverside pools sparkle like small perfect diamonds set in dark stone. During runoff, the river claims the pools and the spring pours down the rock to join the raucous flow.

Linger long and gently. There's no book of etiquette for hot springs, but those who possess a wilderness ethic can spot lots of violations to basic Forest Service wilderness rules: People in the pools using soap to wash their hair, clothing, and dishes. Who wants to soak in someone's used bath water? And even worse— dogs in the springs. People without dogs gag at the thought of sharing a hot springs soak with someone else's dog. Some people with dogs gag at the thought too.

Geology's blessing prevents camping at Rainbow, but the late-summer scent around the camping area indicated a few people didn't follow Forest Service wilderness rules about human waste— bury it a foot deep and carry out the toilet paper (in a sealed plastic bag).

As any Forest Service wilderness ranger can attest, there's steady work in educating the public. Passing along the good word on hot springs care and preservation is one way to thank the geothermal gods.

Heal from the journey and rejuvenate for future forays. Listen to the river's wisdom about comings and goings and not fighting the flow. Cherish the place and the time. As the years grow, so will the crowds. Your time here is the good old days.

The Spa Motel

P.O. Box 37
317 Hot Springs Boulevard
Pagosa Springs, 81147
(970) 264-5910
www.subee.com/spa/home.html
Open to the public; lodging; credit cards accepted
Where: Take U.S. 160 to Hot Springs Boulevard in downtown
Pagosa Springs. Turn south onto Hot Springs Boulevard at the
stoplight (the only stoplight in town!) and cross the bridge over
the river. The Spa Motel is the first motel on the left.

M arsha Preuit swears by the water. For more than forty years,
Bunk and Marsha Preuit and Nancy Giordano have owned
the Spa Motel, pool, and baths. Marsha drinks at least one glass of
spring water each day. "I like it. I drink it hot," she says. Other
folks prefer to refrigerate the mineral-loaded beverage. Preuit
makes no health claims; she just nods knowingly. "When I have a
cold, I gargle with it."

Laws prohibit the touting of medicinal, curative, or restorative
powers of hot springs water. Yet every hot spring has devotees willing to offer testimonials on a second's notice to the effervescent liquid's healing properties.

Marsha makes no such claims, offers no theories or personal
experiences. But she tells of people who soaked horses' legs in
buckets of the water for a faster recovery and surgery patients who
swear that the same soaking got them moving faster. And there's a
man who fills up dozens of plastic jugs each time he visits. "I don't
know why, but people do believe in the water," she says.

. The Utes and Navajos used the springs for centuries. By the
time the vanguard of settlers arrived, the town's name was *Paghosa*,

Pagosa Springs

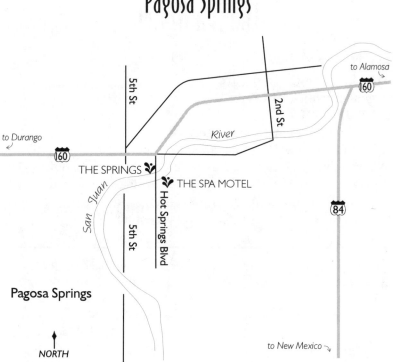

to Alamosa

5th St

2nd St

to Durango

River

THE SPRINGS 💥

💥 THE SPA MOTEL

San Juan

5th St

Hot Springs Blvd

to New Mexico

Pagosa Springs

NORTH

People appreciated the waters of Pagosa Springs in the early 1890s. (Photograph courtesy Colorado Historical Society)

said to be Ute for "healing water." However, the Ute dictionary and contemporary Utes say the translation is closer to "stinking springs," which on certain days is aromatically accurate.

The early settlers said a Ute story described a terrible sickness that killed many people despite the healers' dances, herbs, and prayers. The medicine men called the tribe together down by the river, built a huge fire, and everyone danced all night. When they awoke, the ashes were gone and hot water filled the fire pit. The ailing Utes were cured by bathing in the water.

Regardless of the veracity of the legend, the entire town of Pagosa Springs believes in the water. The town tapped the hot springs using a $1.3 million federal grant in 1980 to build a geo-thermal heating system for ten municipal buildings, including the schools.

The Spa itself is a simple, clean place, not much changed from when the Preuits moved to Pagosa Springs in the 1950s. There's the swimming pool, kept at about 90 degrees, chockful of young-sters on a hot summer day; and the baths—men's and women's are separate—are clean and spare.

The chest-high pools of 108-degree water, sauna, showers, and lounge are a journey back to the 1930s and 1940s, when the weekly trip to the bathhouse was a form of secular communion for immigrants in cities across the country. A time for women to relax away from the children, gossip, share secrets, and snooze. A place for men to relax away from business and family, gossip, share se-crets, and snooze.

In fact, Lebanese, Greek, and Italian miners from the coalfields near Trinidad used to ride the train about 200 miles to Pagosa Springs throughout the 1960s to soak in the thermal waters. Of course, they also drank the water. "Then medicine came along with drugs for arthritis and other things, so they stopped coming," Mar-sha says. However, Navajo, Ute, and Apache tribal members still use the Spa for healing rituals.

Pagosa Springs has evolved into a summer, winter, and fall tourist destination. The environs offer fishing, hunting, mountain biking, skiing at Purgatory and Wolf Creek, rafting, snowmobiling, and just about every other sport except perhaps snorkeling or surfing.

The Spa's outdoor pool is an unofficial adjunct to The Springs' complex of hot springs tubs across the street. The Springs, which is owned and operated separately, discourages noisy, unruly children. At the Spa, splashing, laughing, jumping, and bouncing reign. The daily exception to the pandemonium is in the morning, when lap swimmers churn through the Spa's pool. It's where Marsha starts many days, the rhythm of the strokes moving her through the water. "It's like a blanket that wraps around you," she says.

The temperature-controlled pool is a toasty 95 degrees in the winter and 88 degrees in the summer. The long, deep baths are 108 degrees. The water also heats the eighteen motel rooms. The Preuits are going to add outdoor tubs with spring water. "It's not the same thing as a hot tub. That's just hot water in a tub, but it doesn't have the minerals. And it's the minerals that make you come out with a different feeling," she says.

Her favorite part of the Spa is the sauna, that chamber of solitude and quiet. "You can be stressed when you go in and all. But when you come out, it's not that you solve the problems, but they're not as bad as you thought," Marsha says.

The water's good at dissolving aches, diluting stress, and restoring a sense of well-being. The why is a mystery, despite decades of intense debate by doctors, physiologists, chemists, and less academic healers. "Whatever it is, I wouldn't trade it for anything," Marsha says.

The Springs at the Spring Inn

165 Hot Springs Boulevard
P.O. Box 1799
Pagosa Springs 81147
(970) 264-4168
www.pagosasprings.net/springinn
Open to the public; lodging; credit cards accepted
Where: Take U.S. 160 into downtown Pagosa Springs. You'll come to the only stoplight in the county at the junction of U.S. 160 and Hot Springs Boulevard. Turn south at Hot Springs Boulevard and cross the bridge. The Springs is on the right, just past the chamber of commerce. See map, page 140.

Here is a soaking pool extravaganza. The Spring Inn is growing by two pools a year. The bathing pools are nestled in the hillside under a 10-foot mound of minerals left by the living spring that still spouts from the top. In the fall of 1999, the pools numbered fifteen and ranged in temperature from 92 degrees to 112 degrees.

From a distance, the plethora of pools looks like crystalline green grapes scattered across the flagstone walks, gardens, and fishponds. To the north of the springs is the San Juan River, pulsing with flows from thousands of streams and a few smaller springs. There's a pool a few feet from the river, a cluster of large squarish adobe pools on a balcony, a pool with a small waterfall cascading in. And there's a pool set in a hollow in the natural stone. Each of the pools looks out on the river from a different perspective, and newcomers can be spotted slipping in and out of each pool to find the perfect view with the perfect temperature.

The river drowns out sounds from other pools, especially in the spring. The management is strict about "well supervised children only" and often recommends the separately owned and operated Spa Motel's pool across the street, which welcomes kids and the noise that comes with little ones.

Bathers have their choice of pools at the Springs.

The Spring Inn's pools today are a long way from the four plastic hot tubs the current owners inherited and eons from the natural pools Utes, Navajos, Apaches, and other groups used for centuries before explorers and settlers arrived. The first explorers to the area, who, like most Europeans in the eighteenth century, believed bathing was unhealthy, ridiculed the Indians for their cleanliness. Local Native Americans of various groups shared the spot, believing hot springs were a gift to all from their creator. That kind of community ownership of land wasn't a concept military scouts, trappers, and miners favored.

The late 1870s were twisted times for land ownership in the West. Treaties gave Native Americans the land, but miners arrived to extract gold and silver from the same land and were followed by homesteaders. The military protected the miners and settlers from angry Native Americans who demanded the treaties be enforced.

The saga of Colonel Albert Pfeiffer, the Utes, and the Navajos—with its several versions—reveals the discord that pervaded the 1870s. The standard version claims that the Utes and the Navajos were ready to go to war over the springs, despite their long tradition of peaceful shared use.

Pfeiffer, a talented scout who served under Kit Carson, was stationed in Pagosa with the U.S. Army. He convinced the Utes and the Navajos to reduce their losses by selecting one warrior to fight on behalf of each tribe—a medieval joust in an Indian setting. For the duel, the Navajos selected a muscular champion. The Utes selected Pfeiffer, considered small even in his own time. Pfeiffer opted to fight with bowie knives and made a quick kill either by pitching a knife into the Navajo's heart or skillfully stabbing him at close range.

The longer version includes mention that Pfeiffer had homesteaded in Pagosa around 1865, when he was appointed Indian agent there. By law, the land belonged to the Utes until 1880. And when the U.S. Army moved the Utes out of Colorado in 1881, Pfeiffer claimed ownership of the springs, saying that the Utes had given them to him for beating the Navajo.

There's truth and fiction in each version. But one thing is sure—the setting is breathtaking.

The hot springs are Pagosa's drawing card in the fierce race among Colorado's towns for tourists. The city was the smartest of the hot springs towns, snatching the federal grant to tap the geothermal energy to heat the schools and other city buildings.

Day trips from Pagosa take visitors to two scenic railway lines, Anasazi ruins at Mesa Verde and Chaco Canyon, the Southern Ute and the Ute Mountain Ute Reservations, the Wolf Creek and Purgatory ski areas, and Colorado's veritable wonderland of outdoor recreation.

"It seems that old Dame Nature was in a particularly fickle mood when she located Pagosa and tried to hide away this great natural curiosity," reads an 1890s travel brochure. "The Great Pagosa, the largest hottest, most surpassingly wonderful and awe inspiring sight in the world. Imagine a seething boiling cauldron of hot water."

From the start, settlers in the area saw a resort at the springs as an economic mainstay. As early as 1858, when Captain James

Macomb traveled through as topographical engineer for the U.S. Army, the springs' siren song was not of relaxation but of commerce. "It can scarcely be doubted that in future years, it will become a celebrated place of resort," Macomb wrote. The Springs has twenty-four nicely finished rooms.

Macomb never mentioned the sulfur fumes. Even today, fie to anyone who suggests that the scent is strong. A random survey of nasal perceptions received responses ranging from "Huh?" to "Oh, that's it." "Mild" seemed to be the consensus around the pools. In any event, the winds usually carry any aroma away from the Springs' pools.

At around sunset the lighting changes the scene. The pools become gemstones. The rivulets on the Great Pagosa turn opalescent. The river becomes braids of silver and gold. And the sky flashes through an artist's palette of colors as the stars rise to the east.

Piedra River Hot Springs

San Juan National Forest near Pagosa Springs
No charge; clothing optional; primitive wilderness location
Where: Take U.S. 160 about 16 miles southwest of Pagosa Springs. Just after the Chimney Rock turnoff to the south (left) is the Piedra Road on the north (right). It's also called the First Fork Road and follows the Piedra River. Follow this gravel road about 6.7 miles to the intersection with Monument Park Road and the parking area. Take the trail from the Sheep Creek Trailhead. To reach the springs is a 3-mile hike round-trip with an 800-foot drop going in.

The archipelago of stones amidst sandy pools warmed by tiny springs and seeps are strung along the Piedra's shore like a string of dark beads. It's a primitive springs, especially if you consider sharing with cattle, deer, and elk a wilderness experience. Those with cloven hooves come for the salt in the springs. There's no sign, so the hoofprints in the sand and the boggy mess in the meadow above are the only hints that the springs are near.

In the summer of 1995 there was also about 50 feet of green garden hose and a bucket, clear evidence of the frequent digging hot springs aficionados do to make new soaking pools with steaming water from the springs. The Colorado Geological Survey reported the springs' temperature as about 107 degrees.

Of eight pools, two were green with algae. Two of the clear pools were warmish and had gas bubbling from the bottom to the top like slow-motion champagne. And two of the pools were dried up. Alas. And not an otter slide in sight.

What the trip hinted at, but never delivered, was the sight of river otters. A small otter colony was planted in the Piedra River. The Colorado Division of Wildlife's reintroduction project in the

Piedra River Hot Springs

538
First Fork
596
PIEDRA RIVER
HOT SPRINGS
536
Piedra River
First Fork
Trailhead
(596)
601

SAN JUAN   NATIONAL   FOREST

Piedra

Horse   Creek

FR 622

(MONUMENT RD)

Elk   Creek

PIEDRA RD

to Durango

Piedra

to Pagosa Springs

160

NORTH

Chimney Rock
Archaeological
Area

A crystal-clear pool at Piedra River Hot Springs.

1980s was successful. Generations of otters have been sighted fishing, sliding down the muddy banks, and cavorting. At the trailhead there's a sign explaining the otter effort and suggesting that hikers look for them.

Which brings to mind the Moose Importation Bill—another DOW adventure in species reintroduction. In the 1970s the august Colorado legislature set aside $80,000 to repopulate the state with moose. The large shaggy beasts had been hunted into oblivion some fifty years earlier, just as otters had been trapped into nonexistence.

One key legislator opposed the moose drive, saying, "If any moose wants to come to Colorado, he can walk here." The moose move won funding. But for several years moose importation killed more moose than it moved from Utah to Colorado. In the first year the anesthesia for transport didn't work. The slightly groggy but terrified moose tore a railcar apart. The next year, the immigrant moose got shots that put them to sleep—permanently. Finally, after the proper dose for a short moose nap was established, groups of moose were moved to Colorado's mountains by helicopter and moose communities were established. Baby moose were born. And lawmakers authorized the sale of moose-hunting permits, which annoyed supporters of moose importation who hadn't read the small print on the legislation.

Fortunately for the otters, they're a nongame species that arrived courtesy of citizen donations. No hunting or trapping allowed.

The Sheep Creek Trail to the hot springs starts near a sign about the otters. The trail immediately goes ominously downward. Where there is a great down, there is inevitably a great up. After about half a mile the trail forks left and right. In both directions the trail parallels the Piedra River. Neither fork is marked with a sign. To the left is a bridge and to the right is the trail to the hot springs.

Along the broad river, anglers cast for fish like magicians with gossamer wands. The sandy reaches of the Piedra are trout habitat sublime. The mile to the springs wanders through glades with golden light filtering through the pines.

At the nearby Chimney Rock Archaeological Area is evidence that the Anasazi of ancient times developed an astronomical system that predicted lunar eclipses. The Anasazi inhabited the Four Corners area between A.D. 900 and 1300 and traded with other groups from as far away as Central America and the Pacific Northwest.

Archaeologists believe that priests from Chaco Canyon, located in northern New Mexico and thought to be the center of Anasazi culture, came to Chimney Rock and built a two-story building at the base of the distinctive stone monoliths. The building was whitewashed, making it visible for miles in the moonlight.

In those ancient days, influential people came from great distances to the observatory atop the rock for lunar events. Recent archaeological work has found a rare solar eclipse occurred in A.D. 1125, which would have surprised the observers, terrified the people, and probably ruined the observers' reputations. The observatory was abandoned soon afterward.

The Piedra River Hot Springs aren't on the Forest Service map, nor are they mentioned in the list of day hikes available at the Pagosa Springs office of the U.S. Forest Service. As a result, the trail along the Piedra is quiet. The path winds through piney woods next to the elegant fishing river. There's no hubbub, just the occasional whiz of fishing lines running through reels.

As on all trails to all hot springs, there's been a progression of people here since the Anasazi and the Utes. First the Spanish, then explorers, trappers, prospectors, and maybe settlers made the trek to warm water. And in the last thirty years, hippies, backpackers, and horseback riders have ambled through. Perhaps mountain bikes, ATVs, and paved walks are inevitable.

Perhaps not. Maybe there will be a twenty-first-century American equivalent of the solar eclipse of 1125 that will alter the course. Or maybe those who visit primitive springs will treat them gently and speak of them only with voices of respect.

Trimble Hot Springs

6475 County Road 203
Durango 81301
(970) 247-0111
www.trimblehotsprings.com
Open to the public; credit cards accepted
Where: From Durango, drive 6 miles north on U.S. 550. Turn
west (left) on Trimble Lane and into the Trimble parking lot.

When Reudi Bear bought Trimble Hot Springs in 1979, he
didn't want a fourth fire to raze the buildings, as three previous fires had done. So he asked Eddie Box, a Southern Ute tribal
elder, to bless the springs.

"People said it was cursed by the Utes when they were driven
out," says Reudi, a former ski racer from Switzerland. He said
Eddie told him that the Utes had called the springs "peaceful waters" before settlers arrived and allowed enemies as well as friends
to visit.

When Reudi bought the property, the place had been abandoned for thirty years, the swimming pool was full of mud, the
springs were buried under junk, and antique collectors had been
ransacking the grounds for coins and bottles. Today there's an
Olympic-size pool with water at 85 degrees, two large therapy
pools at 102 degrees and 108 degrees, two private tubs at 104 degrees, an outdoor Jacuzzi at 104 degrees, and massages. There's
also a jazz weekend in the summer.

"A hot spring is a miracle," says Reudi, who fell in love with
hot springs while recovering from a ski accident. "It's a gift you
can't own. If you look at the history of hot springs, they always
change hands. While I'm around, I'm the caretaker."

Trimble is a lovely, grassy enclave. The soaking pools are quiet
and shaded. Bathers tend to doze or read. The swimming pool has

Trimble Hot Springs

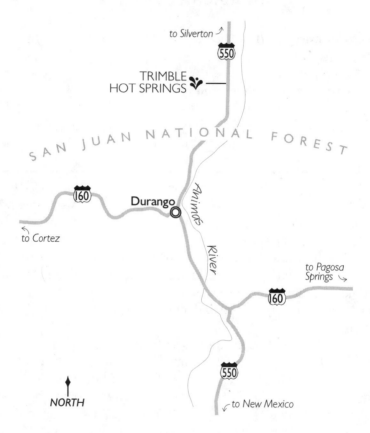

to Silverton

550

TRIMBLE
HOT SPRINGS

SAN JUAN NATIONAL FOREST

160   Durango

Animas River

to Cortez

to Pagosa
Springs

160

550

NORTH

to New Mexico

Soaking-pool bliss at Trimble Hot Springs.

lap lanes, a water-volleyball net and a nice view of the San Juan Mountains.

Reudi grows tomatoes, lettuce, and herbs at the springs. He built an apartment and party room for weddings and small group gatherings but doesn't plan to add other lodging. There's a work-out area, nice dressing rooms, a snack bar, and picnic areas.

The Anasazi were among the springs' first caretakers, building homes and kivas in the cliffs 400 feet above the springs. Except to birds, the ruins aren't accessible today. Only a small section of a granary wall is visible from the springs, but there are more ruins in the side canyons.

Frank Trimble was the first settler to become caretaker, settling at the springs in 1874 and relying on the warm water to ease his rheumatism. "He'd been crippled as a gold miner and the springs cured him, but it didn't cure him from drinking alcohol," says Reudi. Trimble collected testimonials from guests who were cured of liver, kidney, and skin ailments.

T. D. Burns, a successful New Mexico cattleman who started the first Durango bank, acquired the springs from Trimble in 1882 and built a two-story hotel. Horses helped dig the first pool. "A positive cure for diseases the flesh is heir to," read the sign over the springs.

The hotel burned in 1892 and Burns built a three-story hotel, known as Hermosa House, that had electric lights and steam heat in each elegantly furnished room. Hermosa House burned to the ground in 1931. Primitive electrical wiring caused the fires that brought down the two brick buildings, Reudi says, not a Ute curse.

A dance hall went up on the foundation, and in the late 1930s Trimble hosted bubble dancers—women dressed only in balloons that would pop one by one—exotic dancers, and gambling. The audience was mostly local, but the entertainment and accommodations attracted the rich, the young, and the lively. Trimble remained the center of weekend dances and dinner parties through several owners, a sort of Casablanca in the mountains. A sand beach with umbrellas appeared next to the pool after World War II.

In the 1940s, manager Alta Schafer greeted male guests wearing ties by cutting off the ties and displaying them on a wall. Ranchers, bankers, and rascals turned up on the doorstep with outlandish neck gear. The carefree era peaked with a visit from Marilyn Monroe and Clark Gable, who were in the area filming *Across the Wide Missouri* in 1955. And in 1957 the main building burned again.

With Trimble's inflammatory history, Reudi isn't in a hurry to build a hotel near the hot springs. Nor has he been interested in offers to buy Trimble. "I care that people enjoy being here," says Reudi, who drinks the spring water daily but makes no health claims for it. "It's not for sale. I want to take care of it for a while."

Additional Resources

Bud Werner Memorial Library, Steamboat Springs
Chaffee County Chamber of Commerce, Salida
Colorado Historical Society Library, Denver
Denver Public Library Western History Collection
Frontier Historical Museum, Glenwood Springs
Grand County Museum, Hot Sulphur Springs
Gunnison County Chamber of Commerce, Gunnison
La Plata County Historical Society, Durango
South Park Historical Foundation, Fairplay
Steamboat Springs Chamber of Commerce

Bibliography

Abbott, Carl, Stephen Leonard, and David McComb. *Colorado: History of the Centennial State*. Niwot, Colo.: University Press of Colorado, 1984.

Barrett, James K., and Richard H. Pearl. *Hydrogeochemical Data of Thermal Springs and Wells in Colorado*. Denver: Colorado Geological Survey, 1976.

Benson, Maxine. *1,001 Colorado Place Names*. Lawrence, Kan.: University Press of Kansas, 1994.

Black, Robert. *Island in the Rockies*. Granby, Colo.: Grand County Pioneer Society, 1969.

Brown, Dee. *Bury My Heart at Wounded Knee*. New York: Washington Square Press, 1969.

Brown, Robert L. *Colorado Ghost Towns: Past and Present*. Caldwell, Idaho: Caxton Printers, 1987.

Campbell, John A. *Indian Echoes: Tales of Early Western Colorado*. Denver: Marcellus Merrill, 1970.

Cappa, James, and H. Thomas Hemborg. *The 1992–1993 Low Temperature Geothermal Assessment Program, Colorado*. Denver: Colorado Geological Survey, 1995.

Chronic, Halka. *Roadside Geology of Colorado*. Missoula, Mont.: Mountain Press, 1980.

Hall, Frank. *History of the State of Colorado*. Houston: Rocky Mountain Historical Society, 1895.

Hoig, Stan. *The Sand Creek Massacre*. Norman, Okla.: University Press of Oklahoma, 1961.

Hughes, J. Donald. *American Indians in Colorado*. Boulder, Colo.: Pruett Publishing Company, 1977.

Loam, Jayson, and Marjorie Gersh. *Hot Springs and Hot Pools of the Southwest.* Santa Cruz, Calif.: Aqua Thermal Access, 1994.

Metzger, Stephan. *Colorado Handbook.* Chico, Calif.: Moon Publications, 1992.

Motter, John. *Pagosa Country: The First 50 Years.* Self-published, 1984.

O'Rourke, Paul. *Frontier in Transition: A History of Southwest Colorado.* Denver: Colorado Bureau of Land Management, 1980.

Pearl, Richard H. *Geothermal Resources of Colorado.* Denver: Colorado Geological Survey, 1972.

——. *Colorado's Hydrothermal Resource Base: An Assessment.* Denver: Colorado Geological Survey, 1979.

Perkin, Robert. *The First Hundred Years.* New York: Doubleday, 1959.

Rockwell, Wilson. *Uncompahgre Country.* Denver: Sage Books, 1960.

Smith, P. David. *Ouray, Chief of the Utes.* Durango, Colo.: Wayfinder Press, 1986.

Sprague, Marshall. *Colorado: A Bicentennial History.* New York: Norton, 1976.

Ubbelohde, Carl, Maxine Benson, and Duane A. Smith. *A Colorado History, Seventh Edition.* Boulder, Colo.: Pruett Publishing Company, 1995.

Vandenbusche, Duane, and Duane A. Smith. *A Land Alone: Colorado's Western Slope.* Boulder, Colo.: Pruett Publishing Company, 1981.

Wersten, Irving. *Massacre at Sand Creek.* New York: Scribners, 1963.

Writer's Program of the Works Progress Administration. *The WPA Guide to the 1930s Colorado.* Lawrence, Kan.: University Press of Kansas, 1987.

Index